M000286761

No Matter What

May God Bless your Writing

Collette Carlson

COLLETTE CARLSON

ISBN 978-1-64458-534-4 (paperback)
ISBN 978-1-64458-535-1 (digital)

Christian Faith Publishing, Inc.
832 Park Avenue
Meadville, PA 16335
www.christianfaithpublishing.com

Printed in the United States of America

Trust in the Lord with all your heart
And lean not on your own understanding;
In all your ways acknowledge Him,
And He will make your paths straight.
—Proverbs 3:5–6

Contents

Acknowledgment

I Believe
Words and Music by Skip Ewing and Donny Kees
Copyright (c) 2002 Sony/ATV Music Publishing LLC and
Write On Music
All Rights on behalf of Sony/ATV Music Publishing LLC
Administered by Sony/ATV Music Publishing
LLC, 424 Church Street, Suite 1200, Nashville, TN 37219
International Copyright Secured All Rights Reserved
Reprinted by Permission of Hal Leonard LLC

Merl and Collette Schock Wedding Day August 18, 1973

Merl and Collette Schock Family 1986
Children- Jenni, Brad and Mike

Chapter 1

May 1985 – A Reason to be Angry

The tractor roared as she shifted the red 806 International tractor. She was driving down the road to the field a mile away. It was a beautiful spring day, and she had the fourteen-foot disk swaying behind as she put the tractor in road gear. Out in the field, she let the disk down and started tilling the ground. Collette loved farming. This was what she was meant to do. She and Merl had worked hard to get what they had. She thought about how Merl was so afraid of debt and how she had insisted they could make it. She was scared, too, but somehow knew it was the right thing to do. It hadn't been easy, but they were doing okay. They had bought the farm from Merl's parents in 1977. Her parents had warned them about drought, but so far, they had fought the rainy season every year. Last year in June, when Jenni was born, they had fourteen inches of rain. Instead of trying to figure out which roads were open because of snow (like they did with Brad), they had to figure out a way to drive to the hospital that didn't cross a road with flooded water. She hoped this year wouldn't be quite that extreme.

Working in the field is what made Collette happy. She would do her best thinking, best planning, and most praying out here in the open spaces. Collette loved God and believed in Him with all her heart. There was no doubt in her mind that God is real. She felt that she couldn't have gone through one day without the knowledge that God is with her every minute.

A white-and-gray seagull flew over the cab window. She loved the way they would swoop down and pick worms or bugs out of the field, as she disked up the ground. The sky was so blue today. It had white fluffy clouds scattered here and there. It was a perfect day for being in the field, just like so many others. But then, she thought every day was perfect to be outside. When Collette was little, she would walk around on her parents' farm and talk to God. There she came to feel His presence in her heart.

As she turned around to check the disk, she saw it was plugged on one side. She stopped the tractor and got out to loosen the dirt from the blades. She used a small shovel she kept in the cab for that very purpose. For the rest of the morning, she went up and down the field, getting the field ready for Merl to plant. She enjoyed listening to the music on the radio as she drove the tractor.

Merl was at home working on the planter when the neighbor stopped. "Are you going to get the corn in before the rain comes again?" asked Tom.

"Well, we can only try," said Merl as he flashed Tom a smile and then kept working. Merl was a handsome man. He was built small in height but had large muscles on his arms. He had pretty green eyes, light-brown hair, and a moustache that wasn't too long or curly. Collette loved his moustache, and he kept it trimmed nicely for her.

"We're broke down with the planter again, and I have to go to Iowa to get the parts," said Tom.

"Well, good luck," said Merl.

As Tom drove away, Mike and Brad ran up to their dad, and Mike asked, "What did Tom want?"

"He said his planter needs parts and he has to go to Iowa to get them," Merl told his son.

Mike was the older of the two children who stood beside their father. He had light-brown hair, big brown eyes, and a large build. For a five-year-old, he was tall for his age and a bit husky. But he was also very strong. Brad was a thinner build, just fourteen months younger than his brother. He had darker hair and the same pretty big brown eyes.

Brad picked up a pliers from the ground and gave it to his dad. "Here, Dad, you dropped this."

"Thanks, Brad, you know I can't farm without my pliers! It's time to go and check on Mom. Let's go." The two little boys climbed into the old red Chevy pickup, and they drove out to see Collette in the field.

Collette stopped on the end and talked to her husband as the children climbed up into the cab of the tractor.

"You'll have to come home with me and bring the pickup back so I can take out the planter," Merl instructed his young wife. They all piled back into the pickup and went home. By then it was noon, and they stopped to eat. Collette called Grandma and asked how Jenni was doing. Grandma said she was fine and she had just eaten and was playing with Grandpa. Merl's parents, Gideon and Irene, lived across the road in a trailer house. Irene often helped take care of the children so Collette could help in the field.

Merl took the 560 IHC tractor and the four-row John Deere planter out into the field. Collette followed with the boys in the pickup. Brad got into the 806 tractor with his mom, and Mike rode along with his dad. They spent the rest of the day working in the field.

The sun made the day hotter as they worked in the afternoon. At about 4:00 p.m., Merl stopped the planter, and he and the boys went home to do chores. They used the pickup to get the Holstein milk cows up into the barnyard from the pasture. One was particularly slow today, as she usually was.

"Dad, what are we going to do with Donna?" asked Brad.

"We just have to keep pushing her along, I guess. She will get there sometime," replied Merl as he beeped the horn at the older cow.

Inside the barn, the cows were lined up on both sides, standing in stanchions made of wood. The cows seemed to know where they belonged. One became confused, and Merl hollered at her to "go to her stall." She obeyed him as if she understood. The boys helped Merl feed bottle calves. He would mix up the milk and then send Mike over to the calf barn to feed them. Brad would go along and hold the door open for his brother while Merl stayed behind and washed the milk line.

Out in the field, Collette finished up the disking and brought the tractor and disk home. She parked it and went down to help the boys finish up the chores. Brad sat in the barn with his dad. He loved the milk cows. Merl could see how he had a feel for the animals.

"Someday, you and I will be milking together," Merl told his young son. But for now, Brad was content to sit on the bench and play with his little farm toys. As soon as the milking was done, Merl went back out in the field. He planted until it was too dark for him to see anymore even though there was a bright moon out. Collette and the boys helped him fill the planter with corn when he came to the end of the field. In the meantime, she entertained them in the pickup. They talked and boasted as boys do at that age. The pickup cab held farm toys and coloring books and books to read. Mike loved to look at books with animals, especially horses. Even at his young age, he got very excited when the veterinarian would come to the farm. It was his dream to become a vet when he grew up. When there was a minute to herself, Collette would pull a piece of paper out of her pocket and scribble something down. It might be a rhyme she thought of or just a passing thought. When they quit for the night, the house had light in it as Grandma had brought Jenni home. The little girl squealed with delight as her mom and dad and big brothers came into the house. She had blonde curls that she loved to throw around. Her eyes were the same huge brown ones that her brothers had. But hers also had a touch of the pretty green from her dad. She was only eleven months old and was very close to walking on her own power. For now, she used her persuasive powers to get someone to carry her around. Her brothers adored her and wrestled with her on the living room floor as Collette whipped up a few leftovers for supper and Merl fueled the tractor for the next day.

That night after, Merl helped her get the kids settled down into bed. He held her close. Collette's long brown hair fell down over Merl as he pulled her to him. She was the one the children got the huge brown eyes from. She was pretty in spite of the fact that she was overweight. But tonight in bed, it didn't make a bit of difference as they made love with the moon shining in the window. He looked deep into her brown eyes with his green ones so full of love. This was the ultimate end to the day… a day of hard work and happiness.

Their love was real. It was the kind of real love that only happens once in a lifetime. Collette and Merl had both come from humble beginnings. Collette's family was stable, but she grew up with clothes from Goodwill and was taught to be quite frugal. Merl's life growing up was very different. His dad was an alcoholic. They had moved many times in their life, mainly because of Merl's dad and his drinking. When he got drunk, he would sit at the kitchen table and complain about his family. He would be very loud and tell them they were all lazy and no good. In reality, he was talking about himself. Merl and his older brother Larry and their mom would sit in another room and huddle together, waiting until Gideon was too tired and fell into bed. He would make every holiday and birthday miserable, as he did all the "celebrating" by himself. As adults, Larry and Merl bailed their dad out of jail many times for DWI. The last time, he was sent to a place to "dry out." It didn't do much good as he tried for a while, but from time to time, he made the trip to town that brought him home drunk, if he found home at all. The only good part about it was that Larry and Merl didn't abuse alcohol. They didn't want their children to grow up the way that they did. Still, the verbal abuse and growing up in that household left its mark.

When Collette and Merl were first married, Merl would be very moody. He would be upset for days. Collette didn't know what she had done wrong. He wouldn't talk to her. She tried desperately to get him to open up. They were married only two years when she finally considered the fact that they might not make it together. Still, she loved him. Then one night, it all came out. He had come home upset again after a day of farming with his dad and brother.

Collette had supper ready at 9:00 p.m. when Merl walked into the door. She went to him to hold him, but he pushed her away.

"What's wrong?" she asked.

"Nothing. You always want to know what's wrong."

"Why are you angry?"

"I'm not angry. I'm just tired." And he went into the living room and fell onto the sofa.

She followed him. "Are you hungry?"

He said, "Yes, what have you got to eat?"

"I made pig in a blanket."

"Great, let's eat." Then he started to wolf down the hamburger and rice rolled up in cabbage leaves. It was his favorite meal.

"So what did you do today?" she asked.

"We put up hay. Larry came up to help," he said, still sounding very down.

"Was your dad around?"

"Yeah, he was there, all right. The tractor broke down, and he went to get the part. I said I would get the part, but you know he has to. Well, he didn't come home until 7:00 p.m."

"Was he drunk?"

"Isn't he always!" he said with more than his usual disgust. It didn't take him long to finish eating. Then he read the paper a little bit before getting ready for bed. She crawled into bed with him and moved close to him again.

"What really happened today?" she asked.

"I don't want to think about it."

"Maybe you should. Maybe you need to tell me about it."

"You always press me. Why do you do that?"

"I think you need to talk about it. You need to let it out."

"I can't. I don't want to."

"You will feel better if you do."

"Nothing makes me feel better anymore."

"I want to make you feel better. I want you to be happy again. You always come home from your folks so upset. Now what really happened?"

"All right, all right! You want to know so bad, I'll tell you!" he said with such anger that she pulled back from him.

"He almost killed Mom today!"

She gasped as she asked, "What did he do?"

"He came home from town so drunk. I don't know how he drove. By that time, Larry had gone home to milk already. Mom and I were just finishing up milking, so I put the part into his tractor while he stood around and bitched at us. Then he got back on the tractor and wanted to stack hay. Mom and I tried to tell him that I would do it, but he wouldn't listen. He never does. He said Mom and I should go up on the stack, and he took off with the tractor and stacker. So we went up on the stack, and he came back with a load of hay. He dumped it onto the stack, and then he was backing up when he lifted the teeth up and hit Mom in the butt. It was enough so that she lost her balance and fell off the stack. I was afraid he would drive over her yet, as she didn't move at first, and he didn't see she had fallen off. I hollered at him to stop. He didn't pay any attention and moved the tractor, anyway. Luckily, she rolled over in time, and he missed her. I was so mad at him. I wanted to kill him."

"I'm so sorry, Honey. I'm so sorry," Collette said as tears welled up in her eyes, and she reached for Merl to hold him.

He finally let her, and then he held her, too, as tears welled up in his eyes.

"He almost killed me once too."

"What are you talking about?"

"When I was little, he would drag me along to all the bars. I hated it. But I had no say in the matter. Once he was arguing with someone, and I thought he would get into a fight in a bar, so I pulled on his coat and told him I wanted to go home. He grabbed me by the throat and was choking me. The bartender took him off me, and I could hardly breathe. It was so awful. I will never forget that feeling."

Collette clung to him. When she finally got herself together, she told Merl, "God wasn't going to let anything happen to you. He knew that I needed you. I love you so much, Merl. I love you, no matter what."

"I love you, too, Collette. I don't know what I would do without you." He held her close as they fell asleep. The next morning, Merl was ready to face the world again at least for a while. They never talked about the choking incident again. Years later, when Collette brought it up, Merl denied it. He had buried it so deep in his mind again, as the hurt ran very deep.

Their marriage was much better after that. They talked now. They talked about everything. Merl liked to visit, and he made jokes out of almost everything. He could make a funny story out of an everyday occurrence. He was well liked by everyone who knew him. He had a smile on his face and was fun to be around. The years went by, and they bought the farm and had the three children. He was active in church and took his family every Sunday. He became a school board member. He was very well-liked, even when there was controversy. After every meeting, he would shake hands with the other board members and visit with them and totally forget about any disagreements they had in the meeting. He believed it had to all be left at the meeting. He was a man of integrity. He enjoyed children, especially his own and their friends. Many children passed through their home, either as friends staying with their children, as babysitters, or help on the farm. He wanted to do what he could to get the best education for the children in the community.

Farming in the 1980s and early 1990s became difficult. Collette and Merl held on, but they didn't make strides forward. Their prudent upbringing prevented them from borrowing money and taking big risks. So they stayed small farmers. Collette didn't care. She just wanted to live and work in the country. Getting rich was never a priority to her. As long as she had Merl and her family and enough money to keep the farm, she was happy. But being successful was important to Merl, and he strived for it.

August 18, 1993 was Merl and Collette's twentieth wedding anniversary.

It started raining at 3:00 a.m. that day, and it continued until 7:00 a.m. It kept raining on and off from then until 10:00 a.m. When it was over, it had rained 5.90. It had been a rainy spring. In April, it rained 1.80. In May, it rained 5.35, and in June, 11.45. In July, it rained 11.05. Collette had been gone for four days in May when it started to rain. Merl was alone with the kids those days, and he missed her very much. She and her mother went to visit her brother and his family in Ohio. It was the first time in their married life they had been separated for that many days. It rained the whole time she was gone, and Merl could hardly stand it without her. They got very little crop planted that spring. Merl became very depressed as most of the farmers in the area. Today on their twentieth anniversary and almost six more inches of rain, he was especially depressed. The family spent the day hauling water out of the farm buildings. The children were a lot of help by then. Mike at fourteen and Brad at thirteen were willing workers on the farm. Even Jenni at nine years old was a part of the farming operation. They moved the calves out of the water in the calf barn to higher ground. They rerouted the milk cows through another gate and shoveled the water out of the hog barn where the little pigs were. At least it was warm enough, and the little pigs didn't get sick. But it made Merl sick. He was almost physically sick as he watched his family work so hard without getting much in return. He was forty-one years old, and he thought he would be so much better off by now. He was disappointed in life and in himself.

On their anniversary, Collette had wanted to request a song be played for Merl on the radio as he was milking in the morning. But with all the rain, she wasn't able to get through on the phone lines. With the work of the day, the song request was forgotten. That night, when they finally got to milk the cows in the evening, they heard the song come on the radio in the barn. It was "There's No Way" by Alabama. This was their song, and they knew they couldn't make it without each other.

Jenni had called the radio station while they were outside and requested the song that Collette had wanted to have earlier in the day. That night, as they lay in bed, he held her close again, and they talked about the words of the song. As long as they had each other, they could get through anything in life.

The years that followed the flood of 1993 took a toll on Merl. He became harder, and he pushed harder. And sometimes he got angry. It seemed to Collette to be the same anger that he had expressed against his dad's alcoholism.

One day, as they were working on the disk, he became very angry. He could not get a piece taken off, and he just started swearing at the machine and at Collette and at everything in the world. Collette was trying to help him, but his burst of anger scared her. Finally, he settled down enough to let her talk. She told him, "Merl, you have got to stop doing that. Every time you swear like that, you are letting the devil sit on your shoulder."

"What do you mean?" he asked.

"You let the devil come into your life and take you over when you swear like that. Try not to let anger take you over. It doesn't do any good, anyway."

He stopped swearing at the machine and tried to figure out what was wrong. The burst was over for now. But she saw it many times. He let the anger in his life take charge of him too often. Collette prayed that Merl would understand what she was talking about. She knew that he was such a good man, deep inside. She could see his soul, and she knew it was very, very good. She prayed that Merl would be the man she knew he could be. She loved him so much. She loved him no matter what.

They were not happy with the church they had been attending. Both Merl and Collette felt a need to look elsewhere for a church. Neither one of them could explain it, but still the feeling was there. Every time they came home from church, they felt uneasy, not at peace, like they had in earlier years. Something was pulling them in a different direction. By August of 1998, they decided to go to a country Baptist church a few miles away. This was a larger congregation with more people their own age. The first time they attended, the music and the message were so comforting that they both knew that this was the place that God wanted them, at least for now. They started attending on a regular basis and formed immediate deep friendships with many people in the church. As time passed, they would come to know the reason that God lead them there.

Merl, Brad, and Mike 1997 Full Cooler of Milk!

Chapter 2

2000 – A Shocking Diagnosis

The fear of the impending millennium was widespread in the nation and the world. People were getting water and supplies and things ready for "something to happen." But it didn't. It was just another day and another year. But the year 2000 held its own kind of terror for Merl and Collette. Merl had noticed that his left eye felt like the shade was pulled down, and he could only see out of the bottom half of it. They were in Mitchell one day in January, and he said he thought he should check it out. The optometrist knew something was wrong and sent Merl to a specialist in Sioux Falls immediately. Merl and Collette didn't worry too much about it as they drove into the city. As they waited to hear the doctor's words, they were not the least bit prepared for what they would hear. Merl looked small as he sat in an overstuffed optometrist chair. The doctor of optometry came into the room. He was in his early fifties, not much older than Merl, and he had a very grave face. He paused a moment and took a deep breath and then he said, "Merl, I'm sorry to have to tell you this. You have a growth in your left eye. It is probably melanoma, and you will probably lose your eye."

At that moment, you could have heard a pin drop in the room. Merl and Collette were frozen as they were trying to understand the doctor's words. In those few sentences, Merl's life changed forever. Finally, Collette asked, "Do you mean cancer?"

By this time, Merl had come back to life, and he said, "Cancer, you mean I have cancer in my eye? How can that be?"

Collette was trying not to totally fall apart. She knew instinctively that she would have to be strong for Merl. The doctor explained, "Cancer in the eye is usually contained to the eye, and so it has probably not spread. We will need to do some testing to find out how large the tumor is and more about it. The surgery needs to be done as soon as possible. I can do it, but they do a lot of this type of surgery at the Mayo Clinic."

"I want to go to Mayo," said Merl.

"We will make all the arrangements for you to go to Mayo as soon as possible, and then we will contact you." The doctor left the room.

Merl and Collette held each other as Collette cried. Merl was still in shock and didn't say much. Finally he said, "Who is going to take care of the cows when I am at Mayo?"

"The boys will handle things. I'm sure you won't have to worry. You are going to be okay. I know you will. I love you, Merl, and I need you."

They went out into the waiting room, and Collette called her sister and husband, Pat and Curt, who lived just a few blocks away. They drove over there and told them the news. They were all in shock. Collette and Merl were both very concerned as to how to tell the children. They didn't want to alarm them, but they needed to know the truth. They needed to know it was cancer.

Mike was attending college at a town about seventy miles away. Brad was attending a voc-tech school about thirty miles away. And Jenni, just fifteen years old, was an active sophomore in high school. They called the children together, and by now, they had figured out that something serious was going on. Merl looked pale, but he kept his voice steady as he told his children what the optometrist had said. Merl told them,

"I will have to go to Mayo Clinic to have the left eye removed."

Brad said he would stay home and milk the cows and Dad didn't have to worry about a thing. Mike said he could come home too. Jenni just sat there, swallowing hard. She couldn't believe what she heard. Cancer, how could it be cancer happening to her dad? She loved her dad so much, and she knew that she was special to him. Merl had never had sisters, and he wanted a daughter very much. Jenni was the only girl in the family as her Uncle Larry had three sons.

They didn't have much time to prepare for Mayo and the surgery. Brad was very capable of taking care of the farm, but Mike wanted to help, too, and skipped school to come home and help. The boys felt the responsibility and rose to the occasion. Jenni helped milk in the morning before school when Mom and Dad were gone. On one of those mornings, Brad left for school first, and then Jenni. The road was icy, and she drove slow but not slow enough. About five miles from home, the car slowly slipped into the ditch. The ditch had snow in it, so it was a soft landing, and there was no damage to the car. She sat there for a minute, and tears welled up in her eyes.

"Why does Dad have cancer? Why! Why isn't he here to call for help right now when I need him so badly?"

She prayed, "Dear God, please help me! I don't know what to do!"

She realized that her brother was already on his way to college, and she had no one else to contact. She tried to move the car. It spun out, but then it drove ahead. She kept driving in the ditch in the snow until she came to the corner. Then she turned the corner and kept driving. She really didn't know where she would end up, but she kept going. Soon she came to a place that had an approach. The approach did not have a deep incline, so she drove up out of the ditch onto the road. Once she was on the road, she sat there for a little bit, shaking and crying.

"Thank you, God! I know you are here!"

Later when she told her mom about the incident, she said she spent five minutes thanking God when she got out. Collette said, "You must have had an angel taking care of you."

Jenni said, "No, I'm sure it was God, Himself!"

Collette's sister, Pat drove Merl and Collette to the Mayo Clinic. They tried to make small talk on the way. Merl and Collette were relieved to have someone drive them. They were lost in thought for a time as the five-hour trip seemed endless.

Merl was thinking, "Will it be painful?" He was afraid of needles all his life, and now he would have surgery to remove an eye. How will he cope with it? How will he be able to farm with only one eye?

Collette prayed, "God, please let him be all right. Please let the surgery go well and the cancer not have spread. God, you know I can't live without him. Please, God, please!" Then she glanced at him. He seemed to be handling it quite well. For all the anger she had seen him display in life, now he didn't seem angry. He reminded her of a fighter who had the wind knocked out of him, and he was trying to get back up again. He was still hopeful.

They arrived in the city of Rochester, MN, and, thanks to Pat, found their motel quite easily. That night as they lay in bed and talked, Merl asked Collette, "How do people deal with things like this?"

"It all comes down to faith," Collette replied.

"I thought God would hop in the car and go with us, but He didn't," said Merl.

"He was with us all the way, and we just have to trust Him now," Collette replied.

Collette remembered a song that they sang in church, and she sang it, at least as much as she could. It was "God Will Make a Way" by Don Moen.

The words were comforting, and they were able to fall asleep.

The operation was successful. They removed the left eye. It was a large tumor but felt they had removed all the cancer. There was no need to have radiation. Merl was so relieved, as it would have been quite painful to have this kind of treatment. Neighbors and friends helped in any way they could. Collette's sister, Shirley, and her husband, Delmer, were waiting with supper when they got home from Mayo, anxious to hear that Merl was all right.

In March of 2000, Merl and Collette went back to Rochester, MN, to get Merl's new eye. They were amazed to see how these two professional men could make an eye that looked exactly like Merl's real eye. After it was put in, they went to Burger King for dinner. Merl rubbed his eye, and the prosthesis popped out and rolled away on the floor. Merl said, "Oh, shit!"

while he quickly scooped up the eye and ran for the bathroom. Collette just sat there. People around them chuckled a little bit. Collette was sure they had no idea what just happened. In a few minutes, Merl came out of the bathroom, looking completely normal again.

The year after the operation passed quickly. Merl was so thankful that he was all right and that he had been given a second chance. Collette believed he would be okay now. There was a man from a town close by who had the same operation eight years earlier, and he was doing fine with only one eye. Merl kept in contact with him, and he was encouraging. But he also warned to get CAT scans regularly just to make sure everything is okay. Merl's attitude toward everything was better. He was happy again. But Collette knew he was worried. How could he not worry, after what the doctors had said? It could come back at any time. And if it did, it would probably be on the liver.

One morning, Merl got up to milk early like he always did. He went outside to the barn, turned on the lights, and gathered the cows for the morning milking. As he sat down to let the milkers do their job, "If Tomorrow Never Comes" by Garth Brooks came on the radio. Tears rolled down his cheeks as he listened to every word. He thought about how peaceful Collette looked this morning when he left her. Then he thought about her being by herself. What would she do without him? Maybe it will come sooner than he thinks. He knew he had not told her enough how much he loved her.

Collette got up and went outside to do chores. She opened the barn door, and there was Merl. She could tell he had been crying, although he did his best not to let her see. He held her and told her he loved her. She told him that she loved him and she always will "no matter what." It was what she always said to him.

Merl couldn't help but worry that his life would be short. As the year went on, he kept moving faster. The family worked on improvements on the farm, fencing, and other projects to improve the efficiency of the farm. They checked into buying land, and machinery, buying grain bins, and building a bigger milk barn. They moved Merl's parents into an apartment in Salem. Merl insisted on this as he knew if he got sick again, he would not be able to take care of his aging parents as he had always done. Merl took Collette out to supper. He treated her kinder, more lovingly than he had for some time. But as the fall came, Merl slowed down. He knew something was wrong. Finally, on Thanksgiving Day, 2001, he tried to talk to Collette. He said, "I wanted to take you out for supper last night, but you wouldn't go."

"I would have liked to go, but I had too much to do before Thanksgiving today. Come on, we have to get ready to leave."

"No, I have to talk to you." He took her in his arms as he said, "I know the cancer is back."

"What are you talking about! It can't be!" she said in complete disbelief.

"I feel it somehow. I know something's not right."

She said, "No, we did this already, and we are *not* doing it again!"

It was tough just to get through the day with the family. Collette made the appointment for the CAT scan. The wait for the scan and results seemed endless. Life had to go on in the meantime, but every minute of every day, Collette thought about it. She wondered and she worried. She could see the scared look in Merl's eyes and knew it mirrored in her own. Every night they held each other. It was never enough for Collette. She needed him so much. She needed him to grow old with. Why was this happening in their lives? She just couldn't understand it. She prayed and she prayed and she prayed. "Please, God, please let him be all right. I need him. You know that I need him so much!"

Collette's mother was having some health problems, and they escalated in January of 2002. She ended up in the hospital. They discovered cancer in the colon, and she had a colostomy. During that operation, Merl's doctor called and said they needed to meet with him. By the tone of his voice, Collette knew it was not good. But she tried to be brave for Merl's sake, and her mother's now too.

Her mother's operation didn't work in the three days following the surgery as it is supposed to. The doctors didn't know why it didn't work or what they could do for her now. Collette's family came home to her mother to say goodbye. Collette didn't know what to do. She needed her mother so much, especially now. She sat by her mother's bed and tried to be comforting to her. Collette read scripture to her and held her hand. Three days following surgery turned into seven, and finally Collette's mother of ninety years said, "I'm hungry. Do you think I could have something to eat?" So they started feeding her, and she recovered miraculously. The colostomy started working, and she was released to a nursing home. From there, she made remarkable recovery and moved back home again. Collette was so thankful that her mother was able to recover.

Back home again, Merl and Collette went to see the family doctor. They went into his tiny office, and he was friendly as he always was. But his face soon turned dark, as he said the words no one wants to hear. "I'm so sorry to have to tell you this. The cancer has come back on your liver. It is metastasized there." He tried to explain what that all meant, and it all became a blur...

Merl started taking interferon shots by the end of January. He took three shots a week for two months. They made him very tired and achy, and he couldn't sleep well. Collette's family bought him a big fluffy chair to sit in and sleep in if he wanted to. He started spending a lot of time there. After a while, he wasn't milking the cows anymore. Once in a while, he would go outside to see the farm. It was wintertime, but it was a good winter without much snow. Brad was in charge of the milking, and he did a good job. He wanted to do a good job for Dad. Brad had a part-time job and had already bought a few cows to milk with his dad. It was a lot for such a young man to be in charge of, but he handled it very well. Jenni helped, too, whenever and wherever she could. She was a senior in high school by now, active in many activities. Mike came home from college on the weekends to help. He hated being so far away all week. The whole family was already in tremendous grief.

In February of 2002, Merl had his fiftieth birthday. Their college friends made a special day for him. But he was quite tired when they came home. Collette had planned to have a big surprise party for his fiftieth birthday. Now she didn't know when she would have it. She had hoped that the interferon would work, and she could make the party later in the year, when he felt better.

In March, they went to see the doctor in Sioux Falls to see how the interferon was working. They had all kinds of questions about how to deal with the drug he was taking, and it never even occurred to them that it wasn't working. When the doctor finally said it wouldn't pay to take any more interferon because it was not working, it hit the couple like a ton of bricks. "What now?" Merl asked. The doctor said they could go to Mayo and try some experimental drugs. Merl was ready to try anything. He wanted time. So they scheduled a trip to Rochester about the first of April. Pat and her husband, Curt, took them. There he went through a lot of testing in the course of two days. Finally, he sat down with a doctor who said there weren't even any experimental drugs he could take. Nothing was available that might work for his particular case. Collette asked the dreaded question they all wanted to know. In a quivering voice, she asked, "How much time is left?"

The doctor didn't want to say at first, but finally she said, "Maybe two months or so."

The ride home from Mayo was quiet, except for a little small talk between Merl and Curt. Collette and Pat were in the backseat. Collette couldn't talk. Her whole world was changing, leaving, being thrown upside down. "This isn't happening! It can't be! It just can't be! We were going to grow old together and die when we are eighty! That's how it is supposed to be!" She was angry now. She stared out the window for most of the ride home. Her sister tried her best to get her to think of other things but finally gave up, knowing Collette needed time to process it all.

Merl seemed to be handling it okay. He didn't say much. After he came home from Mayo, they had to tell the family the news. Merl decided to give each of his children a gift. He had loved to collect precision tractors. He had two 4020 JD precision tractors, and he gave one to each of his sons. To his only daughter, he gave a jewelry box that had belonged to his grandmother. It was a pretty wooden box with a mirror inside it. He told each of his kids that he loved them and was proud of them. It was a moment that they would not forget.

By the first part of May, Collette knew it was time to call hospice. The nurses who came for the next several months became close friends. Merl joked with the nurses, and they all had a soft spot for him. He never complained. He was happy for anything anyone did for him. He seemed to be at peace. The pastor from the Baptist church came to see him often. He played songs on his guitar for Merl, and they talked. Merl believed in God. He knew that his sins were forgiven and he was going to heaven. But of course, he was so sad to leave his family and everyone he loved behind.

"I want to go instead of you," said Collette. "You get to go to heaven, and I'm stuck here in hell."

"You have to stay because you will keep the family together," Merl said.

"No, it will all fall apart without you! I need you! You can't leave me! You promised Dad you would take care of me," Collette cried as she couldn't accept it. She wouldn't accept it.

Merl tried to calm her fears. They talked about how to keep the farm going. Merl was still trying to take care of his family as his health was rapidly deteriorating.

One day, Merl got a call from Joe, his niece's husband. Joe had given Merl and Collette frequent flyer miles to come and see him and Char in Florida for Merl and Collette's twenty-fifth wedding anniversary in 1998. With some money given from Collette's family, Merl and Collette were able to go on the only trip they would ever have together. It was a wonderful moment in time, and Merl was very appreciative of it. Joe called to say he was so sorry to hear of Merl's cancer. Merl tried to talk to Joe as since that time Joe had filed for divorce from Char. Merl told Joe, "I have to leave my family. I don't want to, but I have to. You have a choice. You do not have to leave. You can stay with

Char and your daughter and have a good life together. Think about it, Joe."

Joe was taken back by the conversation. Later on, Merl and Collette found out that he still went ahead with the divorce. Merl just shook his head in disbelief. He just couldn't understand how someone could walk away from their family. Merl knew that soon he would have to leave his family, and it wasn't by his choice.

In May of 2002, Jenni graduated from high school. Merl was there in a wheelchair. He attended a big party they had for her. It was held in the church basement, and family and friends helped put it on. Merl loved being there. He loved having that time with so many people whom he loved. The cancer was taking its toll on him, as he already looked like an old man and had lost a lot of weight.

The first of June, they sold the milk cows. Dairy had been Merl's whole life. And it was Brad's life too. It was Brad's dream to milk with his dad. Selling the milk cows was the hardest thing for Brad. He wanted so desperately to keep them. His dad knew that they had to be sold, and it was up to him to do it. The man who came to buy them was a good man. He came into see Merl and talk to him. Merl knew it was the right decision and that the cows would be well taken care of. Brad grieved for the loss of his dream. All his life he had wanted to milk cows with his dad. Soon they would both be gone.

Mike got married to Joann on June 22, 2002, at DeSmet, SD. Merl wanted to see the wedding, and he was there in a wheelchair. He would not sit at the front of the church but in the back with Collette's sister Shirley and her husband, Delmer. Merl did not want to go to the reception either. Instead, he went to a motel a few blocks away where Delmer and Shirley took care of him all night until Collette came back to stay. He felt he would be the attention instead of the bride and groom, and he did not want to do that.

Collette walked down the aisle to the front of the church. Before she left, she told Merl that she loved him, and she still wanted him to go with her, but he said he couldn't. So when she started walking, she could not look back. She knew in her heart that this was the first of many things she would have to do alone. When it was over and she walked out, he was already gone to the motel. She went back to see him a few times during the night. He wanted to know how everything was going. He wanted to be there, but knew that he couldn't. Collette felt so torn. She wanted to be with Merl, but she wanted to be at the wedding too.

The place for the reception was quite crowded, and there was only a small dance floor. Collette requested a song be played for the father-bride/mother-groom dance. When the DJ played "Holes in the Floor of Heaven" by Steve Wariner, they walked out on the floor as the crowd quieted down. Joann's mother had passed away from cancer when Joann was about fifteen years old. Mike was about to lose his dad. It was an emotional time for all of them. But the words of the song were healing. They could feel loved ones in heaven watching this beautiful wedding day.

The next morning, they went home from the motel, and as Collette was driving, she realized that Merl was too heavy for her to get into the house by herself. She did not know what she would do, as Brad and Jenni were still at DeSmet. So she prayed all the way home. When they got into the yard, the neighbors Tom and Mary were just driving by coming home from church. So she waved them down, and they came over and helped get him into the house. Collette knew it was an answer to prayer. Merl was extremely tired but happy that he could see the wedding and thankful to be home.

At Mike's wedding, Collette had mentioned to her college friends that the house was so hot and she thought the air conditioner didn't work. So the college friends and Pat and Curt purchased an air conditioner for them. The Monday after the wedding, Ken and his two sons came out with two air conditioners to put into the house to keep Merl cool until the new air conditioner could be purchased. Merl looked pretty tough by this time, and the sons were not sure they wanted to go into the room of this very ill man. But with Ken's coaxing, they came into the room, and Ken told his sons they were doing God's work.

Summer days in South Dakota can be very warm. At first, Merl was interested in what was going on outside, but as time went on, he looked outside less and less. He could not take the heat very well, and he was getting closer to letting go of this life. He had made it to Mike's wedding. That had been a goal for him. Now it was over, and he wondered how soon the end would come.

Schock Family 2001 Jenni, Collette, Merl,
Mike and Brad Photo courtesy of AMPI

Chapter 3

August 2002 – Saying Goodbye

The days and nights that followed ran into each other. Collette kept telling Merl that he had to make it to their anniversary on August 18. She told him she could not bear to go through that day without him.

Collette took care of Merl and hardly left his side. Jenni was there for both Merl and Collette that summer. She ran errands, did chores, made meals, and relieved her mom when she needed to. The boys took care of the farm, but it was extremely hard for them to see Dad. He was changing now. He was very, very thin, and did not even look like himself. Collette brought out all the pictures she had taken of their life together. She tried to tell Merl that he had a good life. She had told him that many times in the course of their lives together. But so often he did not see it that way. She wondered what he was thinking now. He told her every day that he loved her. He apologized for not being what she needed in her life. She told him he was just what she needed. And she apologized to him for not being what he needed. He said she was all he ever needed and more. It was total forgiveness and unconditional love. Merl knew that if God can forgive him, he needs to forgive those around him too. One day, Merl and Collette were sitting in the bedroom. A very thin Merl was sitting on the bed, quiet as usual. Collette never could stand the quiet. She hated the TV in the room because it took Merl away from her for what little time was left. Merl's parents had just left. Collette asked, "Has your dad ever asked for forgiveness for all the years of alcoholism?"

Merl said, "No, but I already forgave him." Collette cried. She was so proud of her husband. He had become the man she always knew he was deep inside.

Merl's only brother Larry came to see him about once a week. It was Collette that called him and told him to come. It became very hard for Larry to see his brother deteriorate so quickly. After a couple of months of this, Collette didn't call Larry to come. When he finally called, three weeks later, Collette said, "So you didn't forget about us after all!"

"I know it has been a while," Larry said.

"Do you know how long it has been?" Collette asked.

"Yes, it's been three weeks," he said.

"It's been three very long weeks. I know this is hard for you, but it's hard for all of us. He needs you, and there isn't much time left," she said.

After that, he came without being called.

Collette's family came often to take care of Merl, bring food, and do whatever they could to keep Merl comfortable. Collette's sister Pat often said she felt they were walking on "holy ground" when they went into Merl's room. It was evident that Merl had angels, the Holy Spirit; something was there with him, waiting for the right time to take him home, giving Merl peace and comfort.

Merl's aunts and uncles came to see him. They told him how proud of him they were and that they loved him. They were inspired by his good attitude and his deep faith. They also felt a special peace in the room with Merl. They cried when they left.

Almost every day, someone from Sun Prairie Church would either come over with food or call or e-mail. There were also people from Trinity Lutheran Church and neighbors who came. They brought food, played music for Merl and, and gave love and support to a family in tremendous grief. And Collette's eyes were opened. She now knew that the reason they felt they must leave Trinity Lutheran Church was they needed the Sun Prairie family to support them through all of this. The people of Trinity were there for them too. You can't have too many people love you and support you at a time like this. God knew how deep their grief would be, and he sent many angels to watch over them that summer.

But Collette didn't make it easy for him to go. She knew in her heart that in his times of terrible pain, she should tell him it's okay for him to go. But it was not okay for him to go. She needed him so very much. She needed him "no matter what"— no matter how poor they are or how sick he gets. She needed him and loved him.

August 18, 2002 finally came. They celebrated their day with roses, balloons, and cake. Their friends LaVetta and Gayle came, and they had a great time together. The kids gave them a plaque that said, "I can do all things through Christ, who strengthens me." Collette read love letters to Merl that he had written to her before they were married, and some she had replied. She also read the notebook from when they first got married and had written notes to each other. They listened to their wedding ceremony on tape from twenty-nine years ago. It was a wonderful day for them to share. Collette told her friend, LaVetta, "I'm so happy for one more day with Merl, but I know it's one day closer to losing him."

As the days of August disappeared, Merl grew weaker. He knew the time was near, and he wanted to "go home to heaven." His pain would be under control for a while, and then out of nowhere, it would come back with fierce vengeance. His level of morphine grew until he was taking 1250 mg of morphine at a time. His liver was not processing the drugs.

As Collette saw the pain he was going through, it reminded her of Christ's suffering on the cross. How great a sacrifice Jesus had made for her, for Merl, and for all of us. She was so thankful to Him, as she knew that soon, very soon, Merl would be in the presence of God, free of all pain and suffering.

Finally, he was in such tremendous pain that Collette called the ambulance, and he was taken to the Mitchell hospital. There the doctors and staff did not know what to do for him. There were no drugs that would take away the kind of pain he was having. His liver would not process the drugs. He lay on the bed, shaking in tremendous pain. Collette cried and cried, "Do something! Please do something. He can't take it anymore!"

So they called the anesthesiologist, and he came and said he can give him something that would make him go to sleep. His brain would think that he was not in pain, and he wouldn't feel it anymore, but he wouldn't wake up again. Merl was ready for it. He could not take it anymore. So as Collette cried and said, "I love you," over and over to Merl, they gave him the medicine. His last words were that he loved her too. Then his body went limp, and he was peaceful. Jenni came later and stayed at the hospital with Collette. The boys came up to see him one last time that evening. His mother and father, brother, and sister-in-law came too. All they could do now was wait. Wait for the end.

The family left except for Collette and Jenni. Collette crawled into the bed with Merl and rested there but didn't sleep. Jenni found another bed across the hall in the hospital, and she rested for a few hours. Then they switched, and Collette rested for a couple of hours. When she woke up in the morning, she felt an urgency to take a shower and get cleaned up. So she hurried and showered and told Jenni to shower, too, as it was already 7:00 a.m. Then she went over to Merl. His breathing was slower and slower. She leaned over him to watch him breathe. Collette told him, "I'm here now." A nurse came into the room. She was watching with Collette when Merl took his last breath. Collette knew his Spirit left his decaying body. Just then Jenni came out of the shower and came over to them. Collette and Jenni held each other as they cried. Then Collette walked over to the window. She saw the sun coming up. It was so bright. She had never seen a sunrise that bright before. She knew that Merl was going home to heaven. The pain in her heart was so great. She needed him. She loved him so very much. How was she going to go on without him? She had three children who still needed their dad so much in life. How would she cope with the pain that their children would endure?

She felt a presence in the room. As a small child, she had feared death, and especially cancer. Now she felt none of that fear that she had always expected. It was as if he was still there with her, somehow. She couldn't explain it. She felt angels on her shoulder, watching her, going with her every move she made. There was a peace, a comfort, as if God Himself was holding her in His arms.

Later, she was driving home from Mitchell, and Jenni was following in her car. The sun had gone away, and it started to rain. It rained over five inches that day. As the rain came pouring down outside the car, the tears that flowed down her cheeks inside the car created an even greater flood. When you have married your soul mate, how can you let him go? How did it all happen? Part of her could not believe what just happened. Yet she knew it was true. Merl was gone. He was gone to heaven. Of that, she was sure. She cried out to God.

"You have him now, but I still need him so much! So very much! Was I so bad that you took him from me? Why did this happen?" She felt as if her heart was torn out.

When she got home, Mike was there, but Brad was not. He had gone to work at his job with a vet. Collette was so upset! She needed her kids there with her. But Brad's grief was so great, he could not stay there and cry. He had to go and work. It was the only thing he knew to do. Mike and Jenni and Collette cried together. The loss was so great.

Matt, Jenni's friend, lived a mile away from the Schock Farm and had seen their two cars drive by that morning. Matt just knew what had happened, and he got in the car and came right over. His father, Roger, followed. Curt and Pat came too. The hospice nurses came and took the hospice bed back, and Pat and Curt helped put the bed back into Collette's room. When night came, she fell into the bed and slept. She was totally exhausted. The days that followed were long, hard days. They planned the funeral, most of which Collette had planned before. She knew that she would not be able to think when it did happen, so she had worked on it from time to time beforehand. Now she was so thankful that she had.

The funeral was on Labor Day. Collette felt like it took everything she had to get the family to the church that day. When they got there, the church was filled with people she and Merl loved who were lined up all along the hallways. The undertaker slipped her the wedding ring from Merl's finger, and she knew it was time to go. So she told her children, "We are going to do this!" Collette walked in with Brad and Jenni. Mike and Joann followed behind. As they walked in, they heard the song "Oh, How He Loves You and Me." The service had beautiful music and kind, loving words from the minister. Brad walked up and read what he had written about his dad. It took every ounce of strength for him to read it, and there was no dry eye left in the church when he was done.

Brad's Tribute to Dad

My Dad always said that wealth is measured in two ways. Number one in money but, most important of all, in the amount of friends and family you have. From the looks of this church, my dad was a very wealthy man.

I thought of some words that would describe my dad: #1 – Education. He served on the school board for fifteen years. His decisions weren't always easy, but he always stood up for what was right. When he made a decision, he thought of all the kids. #2 – A Real Farmer. Dad didn't always lead on to it, but deep inside he loved working with animals and tilling the soil. Being a farmer, he knew what hard work was, and he knew when things needed to be done. Working from five thirty in the morning till midnight was a regular day for my dad. #3 – Family Man. Being a milker, we didn't always get to go on vacations, and Dad couldn't always be at our games or other events, but we did other things together like go out for ice cream, go to farm sales and movies to name a few. Dad helped raise us kids to be kind, decent human beings—to be considerate to others and always stand up for what's right. Thanks for always being a great father to us. And #4, the one that stands out the most in my mind—A Hero. I can remember growing up, all I ever wanted was to be like Dad, drive tractor like Dad, have a plier holder like Dad. I wanted to farm just like Dad. And though I'll never get to farm with my dad anymore, I really enjoyed the time we spent. Even though you are gone, you will forever remain in our mind, our hearts, and our souls. I love you, Dad.

Pastor Mark read what Aunt Ella had written about Merl.

Memories of Merlin as a Family by his Aunt Ella

A family is more than people related to each other.

A family is people joined by shared memories.

Memories of classes, clubs, and trips

Memories of prom banquets and dances

Memories of parents, aunts, uncles, friends, teachers, administrators, and school board members working together to have a better school and community

Memories of church activities that show our love, caring concerns and hope

A family is special people like you, Merlin.

I'm thankful to God for many things. One of the greatest was the joy your friendly smile has brought us. A nephew like you, Merlin, is a treasure forever.

"Thou hast put gladness in our heart" (Psalm 4–7).

Thank God for letting us be part of your life.

You were special to us all.

Mark also read what Collette had written.

Merl's Field of Miracles

When we found out Merl's cancer had come back, people started praying for a miracle. At first I did too. But soon I realized there would be no miracle of health for Merl. I was upset. How could people still pray for a miracle when I knew there wouldn't be one?

I guess I had little faith. But many people believed. My niece wrote us that she believed Merl would grow a whole "Field of Miracles." I couldn't understand where or how there was anything good from any of this. It is all so unfair! And there are definitely *no* miracles! But as time went on, I began to see the miracles, one by one—

The lady who lives in constant pain baked us the "best apple pie in the world."

The day I was so exhausted from Merl's pain and couldn't think of a thing to make for supper, a neighbor showed up with a delicious casserole.

My sister and brother-in-law who took us to Rochester and were with us when we heard those awful words, "I'm sorry, there's nothing we can do."

The neighbor who is struggling with cancer herself baked us an angel food cake, twice.

All the great friends who helped make Jenni's graduation party a success when I could hardly think anymore.

The FFA Benefit and Trinity AAL Benefit that humbled us so much by this very generous community.

The friends who came and played beautiful music for Merl.

The cousins who came to visit, creating a chance to become reacquainted, bringing comfort from the experience of pain in their own lives.

The friends who not only planted our crops but took care of them all season too.

The wonderful man who bought our dairy cows and took the time to come in and visit with Merl so he and Brad would feel better about selling them.

The many, many cards and words of comfort from so many loved ones, especially the "stubborn cousin" who continued to send an uplifting letter every two weeks or so.

The friends who helped make the potato salad for the rehearsal supper when I was running on so little sleep.

The comforting cards from people we have never met that live in Medford, Wisconsin.

The friends who brought us two air conditioners when ours broke down so that Merl could be comfortable

Merl attending Mike and Joann's wedding when he was already very sick.

My sister and brother-in-law who took care of Merl so I could be at the reception.

The friend who took over at the last minute when Mike and Joann needed an organist.

The neighbors who just happened to be driving by when I brought Merl home from the wedding and couldn't get him out of the car by myself.

E-mails and phone calls that got us through very dark days.

The hospice nurses who traveled on the journey with us.

These are all miracles, and there are many more. They are *miracles of love* that we give to each other. Merl's illness touched a lot of people's lives. His suffering reminded us of Jesus suffering on the cross for us. And because Jesus suffered, died, and rose again, we all have eternal life. And that is the *greatest miracle* of all.

When they had the committal service, Jenni's friend Becky played "Amazing Grace" on her trumpet. She was a junior in high school and did an amazing job. She was to represent all the young people in Merl's life. All the kids' friends, babysitters, bale haulers, bean walkers, and all the McCook Central students that he had served fifteen years of school board were represented by this young girl. When the day was over, the family was emotionally drained.

Jenni's high school graduation May 2002

Chapter 4

September 2002 – After the Funeral

The next day after the funeral, Jenni had to leave to go to college. Collette told her that it would be like she was going to camp for a week. She would make it through the week and come home on the weekend. Jenni cried all the way to Brookings. How would she be able to go to school after a summer like this? It is supposed to be the best time of her life, and she was miserable.

Mike and Joann left for Brookings in their own car. That left Brad and Collette. Brad worked in Mitchell for a vet. So he also left. Collette was alone. She didn't know what to do. She just sat down and cried. She was a forty-eight-year-old widow. She tried to do a few things around the house. In the past when she was upset, she had cleaned house. It was always therapeutic for her. Now she couldn't even get herself to do that. Her heart hurt so much she could hardly stand it. She felt like she could barely breathe. All she had ever asked God for was to have Merl, the kids, and the farm. With Merl gone and the kids grown up, she was left alone to try to work the farm herself. And she knew it would never be the same. She was so afraid. How could she make enough money to keep them all going? Her children were so young and needed financial help for some time yet. She knew that the boys would help with the work, but to make all the decisions… it just seemed overwhelming. She couldn't think about it right now. She took a walk. In the days and weeks that followed, she did a lot of walking, exercising. Exercise was a way to release her grief. And she journaled. It felt so good to write down all the feeling she had. She wrote,

September 5, 2002

My grief is so heavy. It is such hard work to grieve for Merl. I'm so tired. All I want to do is lay down and sleep. I know that isn't good for me, so I force myself to do chores around the house or work outside.

When the phone rings, I don't know if I want to answer it or not. I don't really want to be around people right now. I just want Merl back. I want him healthy again, smiling that beautiful smile and cracking jokes. I look at his pictures and wonder what happened to our lives. I need him to hold me. I can't stand it; I need him so badly. My heart is broken, and it hurts like crazy.

I can't eat, and my stomach hurts. Sometimes I shake all over. I'm almost dangerous behind the wheel, because I don't think about what I'm doing. Today I paid bills. I hope I got it right.

Music from the funeral goes around in my head. "O how he loves you. O how he loves me. O how he loves you and me."

I feel like I am in a movie. Each day is a scene, and when I go to bed at night, the scene fades to black. When I wake up, it is a new scene. I don't go to bed until about midnight and then take two Tylenol PM. I'm afraid I won't sleep if I don't take it. I wake up at 5:30 and then can't go back to sleep. I have a terrible backache by then because I have been living on two or three hours a night for so long. My body is not used to more sleep than that, and I have been sleeping in the chair for most of it.

The only comfort I have is when Brad is here or I talk to Jenni or Mike on the phone at college. Or when I think about the funeral. It was a comforting funeral with Pastor's words and the beautiful music. I did what God wanted me to do. So now what? Will I live with pain for the rest of my life? Will the music in my head ever stop? Will the movie have an ending, or will it forever 'fade to black'?

For some women, the first wedding in the family is so traumatic. It is the end of the nucleus of the family, when your children are young, sitting around the table. You have a new member of the family, and the family is forever changed. For other women, the last child leaving for college brings on "empty nest syndrome." Collette was dealing with all of these things plus the loss of her best friend, love of her life, and business partner. For a while, it was hard to just get through the day. But she always had faith, and she prayed. She prayed that God would take care of their family, protect them, guide them, and help all of them heal. For she knew how deep this grief was for her children also. And she knew that somehow she had to be brave for them.

The morning after Jenni and Mike and Joann went back to school, she lay in bed. She could not think of a good reason to get up. Finally, her back hurt so bad. She had to get up. She was still so exhausted, barely able to move. Brad was there with her. He tried to talk to her about their future. He was still in such pain from not only losing Dad but also his dream to milk cows and farm with Dad. What did the future hold for him? He was twenty-one years old and had his whole life ahead of him. So why did he feel like it was already over? He felt driven to work, and that is what he did. Whatever chores needed to be done, he did them. He went to his job, and he worked hard. And he cried when no one was looking. Brad's girlfriend of a couple of years had broken up with him in the course of Merl's illness. It only added to his pain. That summer, he had just started to go with another girl, Desiree, right before his dad died. He needed someone to talk to, and she proved to be good for him.

The first Sunday after the funeral, Collette told Brad and Jenni that they were going to church. She said they had to go. Brad and Jenni really did not want to go, but they did. Mike and Joann were not home that weekend. Collette didn't let them know that she had such a stomachache and didn't know if she could do it either, and at the last minute, she almost backed out. But she knew it would not get any easier, and it was something she had to do for the kids. It was hard to be there, but their friends were very comforting. Pastor was doing a new series of sermons on miracles. After church, Collette took Brad and

Jenni to Merl's grave. There she didn't cry. She told them, "This is only Dad's body that was so broken. He could not use this body anymore. His spirit is set free, and we should be happy for him." It seemed to comfort them.

Merl had passed away on August 30, 2002. It was now September and time to cut silage. Plans were made to get the job done. Collette loved her cats on the farm, and something was killing them. Every day, they would find at least one more killed. Finally, they figured out it was the young dogs that were on the farm. So they tied up two young dogs in the trees to see if they were really the culprits. No more cats were killed, but the dogs would cry all night and keep Collette awake. It was the day before silage cutting, and Collette still had not had any sleep. So she got Merl's gun and had Brad load it for her, and she and Brad went out in the trees, and she shot one of the dogs. She did it with one bullet. Collette hated guns and had never even held one in her hands before, but now she shot a dog. She knew that she had to shoot it because Brad didn't' want to do it, and she was not going to ask anyone else to do it! So she did it herself. They let the other dog free, hoping it had been the first dog that was killing the cats. But the next morning, another cat was killed. They knew that no one else would want a dog that killed cats, so this dog had to be shot too. If a dog will kill a cat, he will kill other animals or harm humans eventually. This time Brad was willing to shoot it, and so Collette let him. Brad was now taking care of even the hard things to do since Dad died. They dug a big hole there in the trees and buried the dogs. It made them sad, but they knew it had to be done. Collette had always relied on Merl to take care of things, especially things like that. Now he wasn't here, and they still had to be done. Brad learned from watching his mother that you have to be strong.

Merl's brother Larry and his friend Rich helped them cut silage that year. It felt good to Collette to be out on the tractor again. It was what she had loved about farming. Yet it was done with so much sadness, for she knew that farming would not be the same ever again.

After silage cutting, the days got colder, and they worked on getting the combine ready for harvest. Brad was not sure how to do all of that, but Mike knew quite a bit from being on combine crew for two summers, and what they didn't know, they asked someone's advice.

Collette was losing weight, and the coveralls she wore were quite loose by now. One day, she was home alone, and the sense of loneliness and grief were overwhelming. She put on the coveralls, got into the pickup, and drove out into the field. There she climbed up on top of the cab of the older Chevy pickup, and she reached her arms up to heaven and said, "Why did you take him, God? I still need him so much! All I ever asked for was Merl, the kids, and the farm. Was that really too much to ask? Why did you take him and leave me here? I don't want to be here without him!"

Tears came streaming down her face. She was hoping God would answer her questions out there in the field. She knew He had talked to people in the Bible, and after all, this was an unusual event. She was convinced that no one could feel this much pain on earth the way she did. The day was cold, and she shivered, even in the coveralls. She climbed off the cab roof and sat in the back of the pickup bed. She waited for God to answer her. Had God left her? She tried to open her mind to hear God talking to her. She still felt something or someone with her. Ever since the day Merl died, she had felt a presence on her right shoulder. It felt like she was in a movie and the cameras were on her. Someone was watching over her. She thought maybe she was on a computer screen in heaven, and when she got into too much pain, they would say, "Collette needs help again. Send someone down right away." It did seem to work that way. In the month, since he had died, whenever she needed someone, the phone would ring, or she would check e-mail, and an uplifting note was there. There were still cards and letters in the mail. Sometimes people would just drive in the yard when she really needed it. She was sure that God had not left her. But why did this all happen? Why was she left here and Merl gone? She had told him she would trade places with him in an instant. And she really meant it. She loved him that much, and she knew life on earth would be unbearable without him. But Merl had told her that she had to stay to hold the family together. How could she do anything when she was in this much pain?

She sat there thinking about it all for quite a while. Then the thought came into her mind and heart at the same time, that maybe she was going through all this pain so that she could help other people go through it. Maybe God needed her to do things for other people. She decided that whatever God wanted from her was what she was going to do. So she got back up on the roof of the cab, and she said, "I'm here for you, God. Whatever you want of me, I will do it!" She cried as the words poured out of her, and she knew she was making a real promise to God, the kind that cannot be broken. God had sent His Son to die for her sins. When she accepted Christ, she received the promise of eternal life. This was such a small promise compared to that. As she drove home, she felt peace, a new kind of peace.

A short time after that, she went to the first grief group meeting in Mitchell. The hospice nurse had a friend who attended the grief group meetings for people who had lost a spouse. They had called Collette and invited her to come. She cried all the way to Mitchell. It seemed way too soon to be going to something like this. But Collette knew that it would not get any easier to go, so she went. She found people there who understood just how she felt. They were feeling the same kind of terrible loss that she was. She was not alone in this terrible grief anymore.

There were only about ten people in the group. Each had their own story. They were all younger than Collette except for one man. He came later than the rest. He was a farmer and seemed to be in great pain, even though it was a whole year since his wife died. At first, Collette didn't like him, but when she realized that he was just in such terrible pain, like she was, she understood. There was another man there who was a farmer. He had taken care of his wife, who died from cancer. There was one other woman who had been married to a farmer. Carrie had lost her husband almost a year earlier in a farm accident. Collette formed an immediate friendship with her. The other people in the group lived in town. Each had a unique story. The group got together at least once a month to just talk or do things together. When you have been married and suddenly become single, you don't know how to function. At first, you don't even want to go to a movie or out to eat. This group met at restaurants, went to movies, and even went camping as a group. All of these people were suffering like Collette was, but she needed a farmer to talk to. Only a farmer who worked together the way Merl and Collette did would understand the scope of the loss she was feeling. As time went on, she went to more meetings and activities, and she formed a friendship with one farmer. He was not a rich man, and he understood her fears.

The financial part of it was huge for Collette. She had always paid bills, worked with income tax, and was familiar with their financial status. Maybe that was what worried her. But she was thankful that she knew where all their debt was and what needed to be taken care of. She knew that some women rely totally on the man to take care of all the financials, and she was glad for the knowledge she did have. Still it was scary, but she had always asked God for enough, and He had always provided for them.

A short time after the funeral, the funeral director who had done the service for Merl came out to see Collette. He had been on school board with Merl, and so even though Merl did not look like himself when he died, he knew exactly what Merl looked like and made him look like Merl again. This brought peace to all those who came to see him one last time. All their lives together, Merl and Collette had talked about having a "closed casket." They wanted everyone to remember them the way they were when they were alive and not what they looked like in a casket. But one day in their bedroom, Merl said out of nowhere, "You know you have to have an open casket."

"Yes, I know," replied Collette. She knew that his parents and their children would need to see him the way he always looked, one more time. It also gave her great peace to see him look like he did when he was healthy.

The funeral director had come out to the farm to tell Collette not to make any big decisions for at least a year. He said, "Don't sell anything or make any big moves." She thought that was good advice and years later said that it should be at least two years. The first year is spent doing everything alone for the first time. This may not seem like much, but it is huge to people who have spent a lifetime as a couple. The second year is still a tremendous amount of grieving, just missing the person you had spent your life with, and trying to figure out what your life is now supposed to be. Collette learned a lot about grief. She went to grief workshops, took grief counseling, read books, and attended the grief group from Mitchell which proved to be her best resource. There she watched other people deal with grief. She knew that she had a deep faith, and that carried her much farther than most. Still it hurt. The hurt and pain of loss is so deep.

She wrote in her journal,

September 26, 2002

Another day. Today I was outside a lot, chasing Brad's stock cow, through one fence after another until we finally got her in the new corral by the water tank. It felt good to run. I can actually run, and I was sweating too! Brad and I are good together. We can make this work. We have to. Tonight, we went to a meeting to learn about the new farm program. What a workout for the brain. I only hope I can do all this.

I still miss him. I miss him in everything I do. I think what he would do or say as I go through the day. And I still need his arms around me. We used to hold all the time, mostly because I insisted on it. We heard one time that you should hold the love of your life twelve times a day. I thought if I get one or two hugs a day, I would be happy. He never did hold me enough. But then I required a lot of holding.

My heart still hurts. It hurts for the best half of me; the half that is not here anymore.

I realize a lot of people are single—single in one respect or another. I just never thought I would be. I thought Merl and I would always be together. I guess we still are, just in a different way. A way I don't like.

Today we started harvesting beans. I miss Merl so much! It wasn't this bad when we cut silage, but now it hurts so badly. This is something we usually did together. And I really miss harvesting with Merl. We would discuss the quality of the crop we grew and the price we would get. It was the reward of the year. Now I don't have him to reap the reward with. Working with the kids is not easy, to say the least. They don't understand how we did things and that I need to do things the same way their dad and I did. It is still my crop, not theirs. I just miss him so much. Farming together was such a big part of our lives. How can I do this without him now? I just want to cry out to the clouds, "Bring him back! Bring him back."

I found a card at Shopko today. It was perfect for Merl. But I didn't buy it. I don't have anyone to give it to. Oh, God, I miss him so much, and I feel so alone.

By the way, I still hear the music. I get it, God. I know you love Merl and me through all eternity.

One night in October when Collette was home alone, Jenni called from college. She said, "There isn't much going on here."

Collette asked, "Do you have homework?"

"Not really," Jenni replied.

Collette knew that Jenni was so depressed and lonely. She told her, "I know how tough it is. I'm feeling the same things you are. But if I can get through everything that has happened to me and say I'm not going to let it get me down, then you can too! We are Schocks, and we are tough because we have to be. The weekend is only a couple of days away, and then you can be home again. You will make it!"

After their conversation, Collette hung up the phone and went to the treadmill. She got on it and started singing the Jodi Messina song "Bring On the Rain." The song talked about how everything goes wrong, but I'm not going to let it get me down.

She felt better as she got off the treadmill, sweating and panting. She looked around as she was still feeling the cameras on her.

The boys were helping Collette with the bean harvest. The neighbors and friends had offered to do it for them, but the boys said they could handle it. Collette wrote in her journal.

October 6, 2002

The men around here are driving me crazy! Brad was driving the 6600, and he blocked it up, and then it had a funny sound. I told him it sounded like a rock to me. But he thought it was something much more serious. That evening, he called Des's father and asked him. He told Brad it's a rock and told him where to look for it. So

Brad says it's a rock, and sure enough it is! (I told you it was a rock, Brad!)

Couple of days later, we are trying to get beans out of the twenty-two acres west of the farm. We can't get across the water in the field. All the rain that summer and fall left lakes in the field. So I said we should cut the fence and go through the pasture to get to the other side. The boys say, no, they want to put the corn head-on and combine through the cornfield. I knew by now that it takes an extreme amount of patience. So I said, "I don't care how you do it, but we are finishing those beans tonight, and I don't care if we are out here all night!" By the time Mike got home from the field, he said it would take too long to change the head and combine corn. They should just go through the pasture. (I told you to go through the pasture, Mike!) Then I was at Emery with a load of beans when the big tire on the combine went flat, and they came home with the combine. If I had been there, I would have told them to take the compressor out in the field and pump up the tire every round. There were only three very short rounds left. The next day, it snowed.

October 22, 2002

The past couple of days, we have been working so hard. We had sunshine yesterday and hauled in a lot of loads of corn and finally finished the beans. Mike taught Brad how to round bale bean stubble. Jenni and I hauled in the loads of corn and put them in the bin. By 11:30 a.m., it started to rain. Mike was combining, Brad baling, Jenni was on the roof of the granary, and I was looking up watching her. I started to cry. I just cried and cried in the rain. Why do we have to suffer so much? Haven't we suffered enough this year? I don't understand it, God. What is happening? Is Merl crying in heaven because he misses us? My face was wet. The rain was cold, and my tears were warm streaming down my face. I still think I am in a movie.

It was late in November. Jenni's best friend was Becky, who played the trumpet at Merl's funeral. Becky's grandmother had died, and Jenni and Collette went to her funeral visitation. They walked into the room, and Jenni just glanced over at the casket. She started crying and ran out of the building. Collette ran after her and caught up with her on the lawn. Jenni said, "It's Dad. I saw Dad!"

"No, Jenni, you are just reminded of seeing Dad in the casket."

"But I saw him. I saw him in that casket!"

"Jenni, you will have to face another funeral sometime, but it doesn't have to be tonight. We can just go home."

"I don't think I want to go home. I want to see Becky."

"It's up to you, whatever you want," Collette said.

Jenni stopped sobbing, and then she said, "I want to stay."

So they walked back inside and sat in the back. They cried as the service talked about suffering with cancer. But later Jenni was glad she was there for her friend. As Collette drove home, she cried too. She had thought her own wounds were starting to heal but felt now they did not even have a crust on them.

Collette now looked forward to the grief group meetings. They were scheduled every two to four weeks. She was forming a closer relationship with one of the farmers. One of the gatherings was at Chamberlain. Aaron offered to take Collette along with some other people from the area. It happened that the others could not go along that day, so the two of them made the trip alone. They talked about their faith and how they knew that their spouses were in heaven. Collette knew to let him talk about his wife. She wanted to talk about Merl, and he let her do that too. Because they were in the same place in their grief, they understood each other's need to talk. She could tell that he was hurting just as much as she was. It felt so good to be able to talk to someone who understood. She asked him if he was angry with God. He said, "What right do I have to be angry with God? I just don't understand why she's gone."

"That's exactly how I feel. God is the Alpha, the Omega, the Almighty. What right do I have to question what has happened? He must have a plan. Do you believe there is a plan?" Collette replied.

"Yes, I do. I just don't know what it is.," he said with a smile. He was a handsome man, just a few years older than Collette. He was getting a little bald, with a gray moustache, and pretty blue eyes.

At Chamberlain, they had a good time with the other people in the group. It was a good day to rest, relax, and talk to others. On the drive home, Aaron and Collette talked again.

"Do you believe that someone can still go to heaven if they commit suicide?" Collette asked.

"If they have accepted Christ as their Savior and asked for forgiveness of sins, no matter what sin we commit, we will still go to Heaven to be with Christ. Of course, it is a terrible thing to do, but you can't be thinking straight to do such a thing," Aaron said.

Aaron seemed so sure of what he believed. She was sure God had led her to him to help her through this time.

The next week, Collette went shopping. She saw all the Christmas in the store and wondered how she would ever survive Christmas. She tried to hide the tears when she saw a neighbor in the store. They talked for quite a while, and Collette felt better. Collette knew that God was sending angels to help her whenever she needed it.

At Thanksgiving, Collette spent time with her family. It was just one year ago that Merl had told her the cancer was back. Her family was very helpful, letting her talk about all her feelings. Curt had a dream about Merl in which he saw Merl, and he looked really good. Merl told Curt not to worry about him, he's all right. Collette said she knew Merl was all right. She needed him to come back and tell her that she would be all right.

The grief group scheduled a Christmas shopping day in early December. A large group went and had lunch at Olive Garden. It was a good day. Collette and Aaron walked around the mall together with the group. They had a good time together. The group had carpooled from Spencer gas station, and when they got back there, Aaron's car wouldn't start. Aaron couldn't get the battery on Collette's car to work, so Collette gave him a ride home to get a battery to jump it. When they got there, Aaron gave Collette a tour of his house. She found it so interesting. It was full of antiques. And she finally got to see a picture of his wife, April. Collette was amazed to see that she looked a lot like April. They both were short, had dark long hair, high cheekbones, and big eyes. Aaron reminded her of Merl, too, with his moustache and long eyelashes. Aaron had told her that April liked to take pictures, was always smiling, had lots of energy, and loved to farm. Collette felt like he was describing her. She took him back to his car and went home after a long day.

The boys helped get the farm ready for winter. She had money from selling the milk cows to live on, but she knew she could not let that run out. Collette knew she would have to start a new occupation, new job somewhere. She wrote up a résumé. It's pretty hard to write a résumé that sounds respectable when you have worked on the farm and raised children for twenty-nine years. Somehow those things don't seem to count in the working world.

There was a job at an eye clinic in a nearby town. Collette applied for the job. She was nervous as she drove into town. She filled out the forms, and when it was time for an interview, she prayed, "God, please help me. Only You know what is right for me to do. And no matter what, I want to serve You."

Two women interviewed Collette. She felt if it would have been a man, she would have had a better chance. The women seemed to look her over like her hair was not right or clothes not good enough. She told them about how Merl's cancer in his eye was discovered, and she would recognize those symptoms in anyone who came into the clinic, but that didn't seem to matter to them. Other questions, Collette felt she had not answered very well at all. When the interview was almost over, Collette just kind of jumped in and said, "When you have lived through a year like I have, you find out what you are made of.

And I am a survivor. I have decided I have three goals. The first one is to be healthy. I am going to eat right, exercise, and start taking better care of me. The second one is to surround myself with good people. That means stay in SD and work in the small towns because we have very good people here. The third one is to find a job I am good at and be successful. My husband and I ran a successful business, and I was a large part of why it was successful. Now I have to prove I can do it on my own. And I will. I believe this job is the place for me."

The days that followed were so depressing for Collette. She felt she had not had a very good interview, and it was a long week to wait for a reply from the eye clinic. She wrote in her journal,

> December 15, 2002
>
> *Mike wants to change our Christmas to Christmas Eve day noon, but he is not sure if he or Joann have to work that day. I am so upset. These kids don't get it. They don't understand what I am going through. There is no point in being on this earth anymore. Some days I just want to take some of Merl's pills and have it over. I have never been this down in my life before. I don't know what to do. There is no one to call for help. God has abandoned me. If God doesn't want me, that's pretty bad. I hear he takes almost anything!*

The next day, they called, and Collette got the job. She was so excited! She had only interviewed for one job, and she got it!

God was taking care of her, and she felt it once again. She wrote in her journal,

December 16, 2002

I cried after I got off the phone with the eye clinic. I have to leave farming behind, and it makes me very sad. It is all I have ever wanted. But this is a new challenge, and it will be an exciting one. Now I know that God was teaching me patience and that He is still in charge. I know I need to work at this job for a while, maybe not forever, but for now. It will keep me busy and hopefully keep my mind off things so I can start to heal. It was fun to tell Jenni. She's ready to help me shop for shoes!

I read my grief journal so far tonight. Wow! It is unbelievable what I have already been through. I am on a journey of faith. That is what it all comes down to. How much faith do I have? Usually, I have enough, because I always come back to God, even if I stray for a while. Sometimes I get so consumed with thoughts and wants and fears. It seems to take me over, and I can't think. Then I finally get back to God and realize that I have to stay on the path He has for me. I know this job is where I am supposed to be for now. Where it is all leading me, I really don't know. I just have to go on faith.

December 20, 2002

It's 4:00 a.m. and I can't sleep. I just as well write this down. People who like blue are loving, kind, warm people. Blue is water and sky. They are calm content people who don't get excited easily. People who like green care about other people. Green is grass and trees. They like to watch things grow and are nurturing. I like red, red barns, red roses, red candles, and I like to wear red clothes. Red is independent, bold, powerful, also creative. I like being different than everyone else. I don't want to be "the norm." I think Merl was green, and his green and my red complemented each other. I was such a part of Merl, and he was such a part of me we didn't know where one person ended and the other began. Now I will have to figure out who I am. At first, I just wanted to be part of another person. But I have to figure out who I am before I can be a part of another person again. If there really is another person left on earth for me. I also like brown. Brown is the earth, another warm color. I love to smell the earth when I plow. I believe in recycling. I don't waste anything. I believe God gave us this earth, and we need to take care of it.

As the days get closer to Christmas, I am so depressed. I just feel so lonely. I miss Merl so very much. Jenni is home for Christmas vacation. Mike was home tonight too. I don't know how he will make this farming all work. He doesn't know either. That's the scary part. Everyone is trying to help him. I just pray it is enough.

In college, Mike had given up on his dream of being a veterinarian. He had been given an opportunity to buy a farm a few miles away from his parents. Mike and Joann were both passionate about raising cattle and were willing to buy the farm when they graduated from college in December of 2002.

December 24, 2002

We opened the Christmas cards from the people at church today. In one of them was $500 cash. It was anonymous. I wonder who that could have been. Maybe some people went together to do that for us. It makes me feel so good to think that someone would care enough about us to do something special for us. There are a lot of wonderful people out there who are my friends, and I have some yet to meet.

December 25, 2002

It's Christmas Day… without Merl. All day I tried not to cry. I tried not to think. But I just can't help being sad. It is so hard to do anything. Just to make a Christmas meal today was difficult. Last night "Santa" brought us a hotshot. We found it under our Christmas tree when we came home from Freeman. We think it is from Tom and Mary. That and the $500 really make it Christmas! Grandma and Grandpa Schock came out here for supper tonight. They were so *glad to come. It has been a long Christmas season for them too.*

I feel like I have been grieving a whole year already. I knew last January that Merl wasn't going to make it. I am leaving behind everything I have ever known and starting over. My friend Deanna wrote me that I am so brave and that she couldn't start over like I have. Maybe I can't either, but I don't have a choice.

December 31, 2002

Today is the last day of 2002. I can't say I am sorry to see it go. It was an awful year, the worst year of my life. 2003 has to be better than this. Selling the milk cows was the best thing that happened to me. I don't miss them, and I know this job will be lots better than that. But losing Merl… how do I go on? Tonight is the first time in thirty-two years that Merl and I haven't been together on New Year's Eve. I know he is here with me somewhere. I don't know if I feel him or not. I don't know what I feel most of the time. I just know that I am very, very sad. Tonight LaVetta and Gayle were here. We played cards and games and had a good time together. I am so thankful for good friends. Mike was the fourth hand on cards, and Jenni and Jeff came out too. It was good to be together.

Mike and Brad discussing important farm stuff

Chapter 5

2003 – "You're Fired!"

The new job started in January. The owners and staff were very good to Collette, and she learned quite quickly. She was still losing weight and kept her goal of eating healthy and exercising. She told her boss that she doesn't see anything there that she feels like she cannot learn, as long as they are patient with her. She worked four days a week and had one day off to do some farming. The first week she couldn't wait to get to the day off. Collette and Brad worked all day and then went to Mitchell to get a few things. She cleaned house and did some cooking. It was a great day. In the evening, she was on the treadmill again. Just trying to make a new life was hard work. Each day she would get up and go to work, listening to songs on the radio like "One More Day" by Diamond Rio.

The sad songs like this on the radio helped ease the pain of losing Merl. She knew she had to go through a certain amount of crying, sadness, emotion in order to get to the other side of this terrible grief she was going through. And in the meantime, life had to go on.

Collette asked Aaron to come up and help Brad and her order seed corn on the second weekend in January. Brad had never done it alone before, and Collette didn't know how to do it either. Aaron was willing to come when she asked him. About 11:00 a.m., Aaron drove in the yard. Aaron and Brad worked on corn and fertilizer. They talked as if they had known each other for years. Jenni came home for dinner and met him too. He was very interested in Brad and Jenni and asked all about their lives. After dinner, Brad and Jenni left. Collette showed Aaron pictures of Merl and also the toys that Merl had collected. He was quite interested in them. He asked if Jenni had a boyfriend.

Collette said, "Yes, he's very nice, but he is a different religion than we are."

Aaron replied without hesitation, "That doesn't make a bit of difference. It's your personal relationship with Christ that counts, not where you go to church."

He told Collette, "You don't have to worry about Brad. He's a farmer, and he's going to make it."

They also looked outside at all the machinery. There was a little snow on the ground as they walked around. Aaron said, "Merl took good care of the machinery. It looks good."

"That was because he didn't want to have to fix anything!" Collette replied.

"The farm really looks nice," Aaron said.

Just then, Mike drove into the yard. Collette introduced him and Aaron said, "April and I farmed just like your mom and dad did."

He was ready to leave, and Collette gave him a quick hug and thanked him for coming to help them.

As he drove away, she thought how wise he was. "And how is he always so sure of himself?" she wondered what he was made of. He has to be sent from God to help her. It can't be anything else. Brad said he liked him and that he had a good heart. Jenni and Mike said they liked him too. The next Monday, they ordered seedcorn with confidence that they were doing the right thing. Aaron had given her hope to farm again.

The next weekend, there was another grief support meeting at a farm by Plankinton. This farmer had lost his wife to cancer. Aaron and Tim, another farmer from a nearby town, were going to meet Collette at the gas station again and carpool to Plankinton. But when Collette got there, Aaron was not there and did not go along. Collette and Tim had a good time visiting all the way out there. He talked about how he wanted to get married again too and that whoever he married would have to love his grandchildren. She told him that if he picked someone to marry, that person would certainly love his grandchildren. Aaron met them in Mitchell, and the two men drove together, and Collette got in the van with the other women. They all had a good day at the farm. These days together with other people who were grieving were very important to Collette. She felt she always learned something from the experience.

She wrote in her journal,

February 4, 2003

Today is Merl's fifty-first birthday. Only he's really not fifty-one. He will be forever young at fifty years old. Dani, at work, asked me if I baked a birthday cake. I said no, then we would just have to eat it without him. But mostly today, I blocked Merl out. Just totally did not think about him. Every time he floated across my mind, I would say, "No, you can't come in today." I knew I could never function at work if I let myself think about him.

I went to church alone this week. It was all I could do, to not cry through the whole thing. My friends tell me I need antidepressants. Pills won't bring Merl back. Pastor talked about the Fruits of the Spirit today. They are love, joy, peace, patience, kindness, goodness, faithfulness, gentleness, and self-control. I realized that Aaron has all of those things. Well, maybe he doesn't have Joy right now. I know I don't either. But he is truly a believer, and because he is, he has the fruits of the Spirit. Not everyone who believes has them, only certain people, and Aaron is a very special person. I went to a Valentine's Day banquet in Shirley's church tonight. It was okay, but I really didn't want to go anywhere. I just want to be left alone to cry. It's what I do best these days. The grief group is getting together on Valentine's day night. I hope I can go. At least they will understand how I feel.

February 14, 2003

It's Valentine's Day. We woke up to icy roads and rain/sleet/snow. Early this morning, I fell down the steps outside the house. I called the Cenex and told them that it was a message from God to stay home today. So I didn't get the car's oil changed or the radiator hose put on. I don't have a car that works, and the roads are icy, so I canceled going to the grief group for the evening. It was like God was determined that I stay home tonight. He sent a storm, broke my car, and if that wasn't enough, he knocked me on my butt too. But in the evening, Mike and Joann came over, and Brad and Des were here, so I wasn't alone. I am so thankful for my kids. It was so good to be with them. I guess maybe He knows what He's doing after all.

February 15, 2003

That was yesterday. Today the sun came out. I got my car fixed, and the roads were better. I drove down to see Aaron. He said he had a very depressing Valentine's Day too and went to bed early. We talked about everything. He is against the war, and he knows so much about things. He said the grief group needs to have some fun and not only talk about the sad stuff. I told him that Brad thinks he messed up ordering fertilizer. Brad said he wishes Dad would have lived three years longer, so he could have taught him some farm stuff. He also thinks a lot of Aaron. Aaron offered to come up on Friday night and talk to Brad about it again.

The next Friday night, Aaron came up to talk with Brad. He made Brad feel good again about farming. Brad just needed some encouragement, and Aaron's mission right now was to give him that. They had a good time visiting, and when Brad left,

Collette and Aaron talked a while. It was good time together. Collette was so happy that Aaron took the time and effort for Brad, and she needed that encouragement too.

The next grief group meeting was in March, a couple of weeks later. Collette went to Mitchell, but Aaron wasn't there at first. He came quite late and was in a quiet mood. Later, she got to talk to him. He said his dad had heart surgery. He did not get much sleep and was very worried about him. He was glad to see Collette and talk to her a little bit. The grief group decided not to meet in April and May, so Collette invited them all to come to her farm in June.

March 13, 2003

Last night, Jenni ended up in the ER in Brookings Hospital. She had a stress attack that felt like a heart attack. Her roommate and friends took her to the ER and Brad and Des and I flew (drove very, very fast) up there to see her. I have seen this coming. I guess I can be thankful that she waited this long. We had a very nice doctor. He said that if she doesn't release stress, it will come out in other ways. She needs to meditate, exercise, and see a counselor. She finally slept when they gave her medicine. I don't know what to do anymore! She won't listen to me when I tell her how I am coping with prayer, exercise, journaling, music, etc. I'm glad the doctor told her those things. Maybe she will listen to him. Today I called at noon, and she called tonight. She is doing better today.

When Jenni came home the next day, she finally talked to Collette. It was exactly what Collette had thought. Losing Dad was just sitting in the back of her mind all the time. The grief just welled up inside of her, and she didn't know what to do with it. She had not told her friends at college that her dad died last summer, and she left for college the day after the funeral. All this time, she had kept the secret. After the ER incident, she finally told them about it. Then they opened up about sadness in their own lives, divorce, abuse, etc. Collette told Jenni that she was lucky to have two parents who loved each other, and their life was good for the most part. Jenni said, "When Dad died, the first thing I thought of is that he can't walk me down the aisle when I get married. I don't know who I would ask or who would do that for me now."

"Don't think about that now. We will worry about that when the time comes," Collette said.

Collette told Jenni, "I can't fix this for you. I wish I could, but I can't. All I can do is love you."

They had a good talk and good time together over the weekend. Sunday night, Jenni was ready to go back to school and face life again.

The next morning, Collette finally told Brad that Aaron's dad had heart surgery. She said, "I hope Aaron doesn't lose his dad now. It would be like losing his best friend."

The look on Brad's face was as if he had just been shot. He didn't say anything. Finally, Collette said, "You know exactly what that is, don't you?"

Brad said, "Yes," and then he quickly left for work, afraid he would shed tears in front of Mom. He always wanted to appear tough and brave.

The night before, Collette had asked Mike, "Do you think about Dad?"

Mike said, "Yes."

Collette asked, "Do you miss him, or do you think about how he was a pain sometimes?"

Mike answered, "The latter."

Being the oldest in the family, Mike had seen his dad's bursts of anger more than the other children when he was growing up. Collette knew that her children were still in so much pain. She just didn't know what to do to make it better.

Collette tried to call Aaron and tell him about Jenni's stress attack, but he didn't answer the phone for several days. So on her next day off, she drove to his farm and stopped in on the way to her mother in Freeman. By the time she got there, she almost lost her nerve to stop. She didn't want to surprise him if he didn't appreciate it. She played with the dog, as she slowly walked up to the house. After she finally knocked, he answered the door. He had just got out of the shower and was still wet, drying off his chest with a towel and wearing blue jeans. She thought he looked very handsome and didn't know what to say at first. Finally, she blurted out, "I was on my way to Mom today and thought I would stop in. You didn't answer the phone the last few days, and I thought maybe something happened to your dad."

"Come on in," he said. "No, Dad is okay. I was out at Sturgis. My daughter was in the Junior Miss contest."

They talked for an hour. She told him about Jenni's stress attack and her children's grief. He said he just can't get his income tax done. Collette said, "You not doing income tax is like me checking oil on the car. I refuse to do it because Merl was supposed to check oil and keep the car going for me. I'm sure April was the one who did the taxes for you too. Doing those things is like accepting they are not here. There is a place deep inside of us that just doesn't want to accept that just yet. But we will. Eventually, we will."

They made plans for Aaron to come up to see Collette the next week and help Brad order alfalfa. But when the day came, he called and said he couldn't come. She was disappointed. He was always the bright spot in the day when he came to see her.

Every day she drove to work, she would listen to songs on the radio and try to get herself together. She did not enjoy her job but tried her best to learn it, as she appreciated the chance to have it.

She wrote in her journal,

April 2, 2003

I was so depressed tonight I couldn't take it anymore. No one was home, and I just felt so alone. It was about 9:30 when I put on Merl's coat, took the flashlight and my cellphone, and started walking in the dark. I walked past Grandpa's and went south. I stopped once and looked back at the farm. Then I turned around and went south again. My feet slopped along on the gravel. It was cold, dark, and very windy. I walked almost to the half-mile gate, and then I finally cried and cried and cried. I wanted to keep walking until I just fell down and lay there until morning. But then I knew that my kids would cry. And it's bad enough that I cry. I don't want my kids to cry like this too. So I turned around and started coming back. At first, I didn't even know where I was. My tears blinded me. But I made it into Grandpa's yard and sat down by a round hay bale, just east of the garage. I don't have Merl, I can't farm, and I feel so alone. I sat there a long time and got so very cold. Finally, I called Larry's cell number. I told him I was so depressed and that I was out in the bales at Grandpa's. He kept telling me to go home where it was warm. He seemed concerned. I told him about the man who came into the eye clinic today. He was in a wheelchair, about Merl's age and very good-natured. When I saw him, tears welled up, and I couldn't wait on him. I went down the hall, and it was all I could do not to totally fall apart. When he was done, I had to wait on him to pay his bill too. He was a very nice man, and he had MS. When I got off the phone with Larry, I still sat there awhile. I was too cold to go home against the wind. Finally, I just knew I had to go back home. When I got back, I lay down on the couch with Merl's coat on and a blanket. I was still so cold. I think I might have fallen asleep. After a while, the phone rang. I didn't get up to answer it, and no one left a message. I knew it was Larry. Then my cell phone rang, and it was Larry. He wanted to know if I made it home. I told him I was on the sofa with Merl's coat and a blanket. He seemed relieved. He said he would call tomorrow. (He never called.) I am so broken. I feel like a piece of fine china that has fallen on the floor into a million pieces. I guess maybe I have finally given up on the dreams we had. If you don't have dreams, you have nothing. Your life is empty. I guess empty is exactly how I feel. And I ache. My heart aches all the time. I want to cry all the time. Is this never going to quit? I feel like I will be alone the rest of my life. I can't imagine there being anyone for me in this life. I will be unhappy the rest of my life. The only way I can be happy is to share life with someone. Some people can be fulfilled by being their own person. But I need to be part of someone else in order to be whole. Merl and I had that. Maybe it is true that you only get one true love in your life. So why did mine have to die so early? Why am I being punished? I thought God didn't work that way.

April 4, 2003

I found over $150 in a drawer today. I know Merl stashed this money to buy me flowers or little gifts for Valentine's Day, etc. I cried again. Then I was cleaning my closet and saw Merl's shirts. I held one and smelled it. I cried again. I feel so empty. I thought I had moved on a bit, but I guess not. I guess this is one of those valleys they talk about. I feel like I have nothing to look forward to. Mike and Brad are exhausted. They are trying to work themselves to death. I think they figure they won't feel anything if they just work until they are exhausted. I *try to send e-mails to Jenni to encourage her and keep her going, make her laugh if I am lucky. But I really don't feel it. Aaron called tonight. Earlier, he had said he would come tonight, but when he called, he was very sad about it, but he can't come tonight. He didn't get home until very late last night, had company most of the morning, and still has income tax to do. I told him it is like we live 1,000 miles apart. Hopefully, he can come on Monday night, but there is snow predicted.*

April 7, 2003

Mike came over today, and we were going to load up the last cornstalk bales so he could take them home. Mike took the 1086 and loader out on the road. He didn't get very far when Brad and I heard a loud noise and a screech. We didn't know what it was at first, and Brad got so upset. He got in his '93 Lumina and tore out of the yard that the gravel was just flying behind him. When the dust cleared, he was in the ditch across the road. He said it locked up, he couldn't stop or turn, so it flew across the ditch. The nose of the car was on the other side of the ditch, and the back of the car was on the road and the rest of it on tree branches that were laying horizontal in the ditch. He got out of the car, and the bottom of the car was up to his waist in the ditch. He was so mad! He started walking down the road south to Grandpa's. Mike saw what happened and came running down the road to see if he was all right. The front tire on the 1086 had blown out. Mike got it off the road so it could be changed. I had just had a session with Brad that morning about anger. Brad's anger is just taking him over. I realize that he is angry that Dad is not here, but anger doesn't fix anything. It only makes it worse, as he can see now. We pulled the car out of the ditch, changed the tire on 1086, hauled bales, and then Brad and I headed for Brookings. Jenni got her first place proficiency and looked so happy tonight at the FFA Convention. Brad told Jenni about his accident, and she just laughed and laughed. We left as soon as we could because it was snowing at home. I drove all the way up and back. Brad kept after to me to let him drive. I said, "Hell, no!" We ran into snow about five miles north of Madison. It didn't get really bad until a few miles north of the Unityville Road. I could barely see to make the turn to get home. Brad said I was giving him an ulcer. Better him than me. He would have tried to drive 60 mph on 35 mph road conditions! We got home at 11:00 p.m. I was totally exhausted. Mike and Joann were here checking our cattle in the snow. They came in for a little bit to visit. Joann thought Brad was so funny.

That was yesterday. This morning, we had about six to seven inches of snow, and then it snowed all day again. But Aaron still came up tonight. We had a good time together. He seemed to be in a really good mood tonight. I think it is very good for him to be helping me with some farm stuff.

A couple of days later, she wrote in her journal,

April 9, 2003

I had a terrible night last night. I couldn't sleep for so long, and when I finally did, I was dead tired, and I had this dream. I dreamt some awful huge man was chasing me in this big building, and finally he gets me and holds me down on the floor and tries to rape me. All of a sudden, out of nowhere, Aaron appears, and he looks so small compared to the big man on top of me. But Aaron chases him away just with words. To me, being raped represents the most awful thing anyone could do to me. I couldn't believe that Aaron was in my dream. I haven't even dreamt about Merl yet. Maybe Aaron is my "knight in shining armor" who has come to save me from all the heartache of losing Merl. I should tell Aaron that I'm not smart like he is, but I do have a gift. I can see things that other people can't see, and I feel things very deeply. When I look at him, I see a wonderful, loving, kind man who is very sad because he has a huge hole in his heart.

The days in April went by quickly. Despite a lot of rain, the boys got oats planted and also alfalfa.

Jenni had developed another problem. She had a bad knee and was on crutches. She went to the SDSU nurse and got it x-rayed. It was not dislocated, but it might be a torn ligament. Collette was as depressed as Jenni was. Why did they have to suffer so much? Jenni had a hard time to get to her classes with crutches, but she tried not to miss them. On the weekend, Jenni came home and went to their local doctor. He said she needs an orthopedic doctor and her knee may need scoping. So they set up an appointment and waited.

The Schock family had set up a Merlin Schock Memorial Scholarship. The recipient had to be very involved in FFA, striving to be a farmer or ag-related occupation, and have done a lot of voluntary service in the community. A small committee had picked a winner, and the scholarship was to be given out at the McCook Central FFA Banquet. Brad said he would give out the first award. He almost didn't make it on time, as he was at work that day. Mike and Joann, Jenni and Collette were all there. Brad said to the crowd, "Merlin Schock, my father, served on the Spencer and McCook Central school board for fifteen years. He believed that students should have the chance to better themselves through activities that teach leadership, cooperation, teamwork, and a strong work ethic. That's why he supported the FFA.

On August 30, 2002, Dad passed away from melanoma liver cancer. He knew that everything in this life can be taken from you, your job, your home, your family, or your health. But no one can take away your education.

Collette wrote in her journal that night,

We gave away the first Merlin Schock Memorial Scholarship tonight. I rushed home from work, did chores, and then went to the school. I was afraid I would have to hand it out myself because Brad was late getting there after work. But he made it and did a great job of announcing it and reading the little speech Jenni and I had written. We took pictures when it was over, and I felt good about it all. I held it together without crying through the whole thing. Then I got in the car to go home, put the key in and the radio came on with this song just starting to play.

"Every now and then, soft as breath upon my
    skin
I feel you come back again, and it's like you
    haven't been,
Gone a moment from my side, like the tears
    were never cried,
Like the hands of time are holding you and
    me.
And with all my heart I'm sure, we're closer
    than we ever were.
I don't have to hear or see. I've got all the
    proof I need.
There are more than angels watching over
    me. I believe. Oh I believe

Now when you die, your life goes on. It
    doesn't end here when you're gone.
Every soul is filled with light, it never ends if
    I'm right.
Our love can even reach across eternity. I
    believe, oh I believe.

Forever you're a part of me; Forever in the
    heart of me.
I will hold you even longer if I can.
Oh, the people who don't see the most; see
    that I believe in ghosts.
And if that makes me crazy, then I am. Cause
    I believe, oh I believe.
There are more than angels watching over
    me. I believe, oh I believe.
Every now and then, soft as breath upon my
    skin
I feel you come back again. And I believe."[1]

*I cried all the way home, but I knew Merl
was there with me tonight. I love him and I miss
him so much!*

(Songwriters Skip Ewing and DonnyKees,
sung by Diamond Rio)

The next morning, Aaron called, and she had a chance
to tell him about Jenni's knee problems and that Brad was so

---

[1] Diamond Rio, *I Believe*, by Skip Ewing and Donny Kees, recorded 2002, Arista
    Nashville, track 15 on *16 Biggest Hits*, 2008, compact disk.

restless and wanted his own place nearby. She told him that it was always something she had to make decisions on, and she's not ready to do that yet. He said he had been to Texas for his nephew's wedding and had a good time but came home with a terrible cold. Also that his girls moved out and so now he had to take care of the house, too, when he can't get the farming done by himself. Later in the day, Tim called just to visit. He told her he was so lonely he couldn't stand it. He just didn't know what to do with himself. His children are somewhat helpful, but they all have their own lives. He told Collette that he knows he should not have a pity party, but sometimes he can't help it. Collette told him that she understands him feeling that way, and it is part of the grieving process as she tried to be encouraging to him too.

Collette wrote in her journal,

May 6, 2003

At work today, I heard on the radio "I Believe." I just had to stop what I was doing and listen. On the way home from work, the car turned and drove to Merl's grave. I had to see it again. They just put it up last week. It looks really nice, just the way I wanted it. It made me cry to see it. I know he's not there, but to see the stone… I guess it is just so final. Not that it hasn't been final before, still, it is so "set in stone." The date on it says February 4, 1952– August 30, 2002. He had fifty years. In the middle are the wedding rings with our wedding date, August 18, 1973. He had the best years of my life, and I had the best years of his life. I guess that is all you can ask. There is still such an empty feeling. When does this aching stop? I know I have to go through this. I can't go on with the rest of my life until I get through this part. And I will get through it because God will give me the strength to do it. In the evening, Mike came over to try to get my dryer belt on so it works again. We were working on it, and the sparks flew all over. Mike was almost the cat on "Christmas Vacation." Now the belt is on, and the dryer still doesn't work. I guess I will have to call the Maytag repairman. At least Mike tried. Jenni got word today that she needs an MRI because she doesn't hurt in the place he would expect, so maybe she just needs medication and therapy. That would truly be a miracle. This family needs one or two or three miracles desperately! I just can't afford Jenni's surgery. My insurance is so worthless. But we would have to do it if she needs it.

May 9, 2003

I went to Brookings today to help Jenni move home. She filled both our cars up with the rest of her things, as the boys had gone to get furniture earlier. It was pouring rain all day. What a fitting end to her freshman year of college. I cried in the rain on the way up and on the way home. Even Jenni was so sad. Her year ended the way it had begun, with so much sadness. We were both so glad to get home.

When Jenni finally took the MRI, it showed that she did not need surgery, only some physical therapy. They were all so happy. They got the miracle they needed. She got into the tractor then and helped her brothers do the farming that summer. She looked so small in the tractors, but she was a tough farm girl, and she just did what needed to be done. That's what all of them were doing.

Collette was invited to Aaron's daughter's high school graduation. So she went to the graduation and saw Tim in the crowd, waving for her to come and sit by him. So she did. Tim had a large farm nearby, and she enjoyed talking about farming with him. Afterward, they went to the graduation party. Collette met Aaron's family for the first time. They were very nice people. When Collette was introduced to Aaron's dad, she asked him where they had met before. She was sure that she had met this man before. He had the same feeling. But they tried to figure out where or how and just could not come up with an answer. She immediately knew his dad was kind, honest, loving… just like Aaron. She liked his mother too and also met some siblings. Tim and Collette were the only ones from the grief group who were there, and Aaron was so glad they came. When she got home, she finally got to drive the tractor in the field too. It made Collette very happy. It was a good day. The next day, the Schock family was invited to graduation parties in the Salem/Spencer area. Jenni's car died, and Collette had to go and get her from one of the parties. Don was there. When they got to the next party, Don walked in to the place in front of them. Collette said to him, "It looks like we are following you."

Don said, "It's kind of nice. Usually women don't follow me!" Don was from Collette's church. He was recently divorced and had known Merl and Collette since they started coming to Sun Prairie church. Don had only one eye that could see. He got a metal speck in his eye when he was eighteen years old. So when it was announced in church that Merl would have his eye removed, Don was the first one to talk to Merl about it. He said not to worry about it; he had farmed for many years with only one eye, and Merl could too. Merl had been so happy that Don was encouraging to him.

The next days were busy with planting. Brad had never planted before, but Mike taught him what to do. He did a good job. Collette did the dragging with the 560 IHC tractor. This tractor meant a lot to Collette. It was the one she learned how to drive when she and Merl first got married. It took her back to those days, remembering how it all came about. They had bought the farm from his parents the fall before, and it was already late in spring. Merl was taking a lot of time, trying to seed pasture for his parents. Nice days were going by, and she kept telling Merl that he had to start disking for corn when it was so nice. In frustration, Merl had told her that if she thought she knew so much, she should just go out there and disk. He was thinking, of course, that it would keep her from bringing it up. Instead, she had answered him in a very excited voice that she could do the disking; he just needed to teach her! Merl had not been happy about teaching her, but it proved to be one of the best things he ever did. Through the years, she would do the disking and preparation of the field while he got the planter ready and came behind to get the crop planted. It was a good memory for Collette, and being on the 560 felt so right. That night, she called Aaron, just to visit.

"Thanks so much for inviting me to the graduation party," she said.

"I'm glad you could come."

Collette said, "You really have wonderful parents. It was so good to meet them and interesting to visit with them."

Aaron told her, "I feel very blessed to have them."

"They are blessed to have you too," she said. Then she told him how they had been farming. He recommended that they roll the beans very soon, since there were so many rocks. He was very encouraging again, and they had a good visit.

Memorial Day was tough that year. Collette went to the grave again. This time, she had on her Ag-Source jacket because it was cool and windy. She cried as she talked to Merl. She said, "Everyone is doing the best they can. We are getting the farming done and just trying to survive. I still love you *no matter what* happens in this life." (Then she wondered why she never remembers to take tissues along when she goes to the grave. And why do the birds poop all over the stone? Can't they wait to go until they are a foot farther over?) "I still don't understand why it all happened this way. I need you here to take care of me the way you always did. Aaron is being very helpful. He seems so nice, but he is not you. I just want you back! I think I will be crying the rest of my life."

May 26, 2003

The worst two days of this holiday are over, and today I was going to have a good day. It was beautiful—70 degrees, and we worked hard all day. Jenni helped me clean up the basement in the morning. In the afternoon, Brad and Des and I tore out old dead trees and the fence around the house. It looks a lot better now. Brad got stuck with the loader in the ditch tear-

ing out fence with Des. Roger (neighbor) had to come over and pull him out. Roger thinks our family is so funny. Jenni is running the disk. She got stuck twice because the mud "sucked her in." Brad is stuck more often this spring than anyone. I think his number is 4 or 5. At least one of those times was with the pickup in the field. Tonight the kids were all here for supper, Mike, Joann, Brad, Des, Jenni, and Jeff. Brad made popcorn shrimp. We even had beer, for once, and all had a good time. I took a walk after supper and then sat outside the window and listened to them talk awhile. They have such a good time together. They plan their work, and they have fun along the way. I am so happy to have my kids. I look at them now and know that I have the best part of Merl still with me on earth. But still, something is missing from my life. I don't know if I will ever get it back. There is a big hole in my heart. I work hard to try and forget it, but the aching still comes back, no matter what. Merl will always have a special place in my heart. But I have to live this life while I am here. And I still pray that God will let me share my life with someone who would love me for who I am. It's 3:00 a.m. now when I am writing this. Time is so different now. We used to be on such a strict schedule with the milking. There was a time to eat, a time to sleep, and a time to milk. Today my watch quit, and I am finally officially a stock cow farmer—no watch!

June 8, 2003

Today the grief support group came here. There were seven of us today. The three farmers came and the three women I am the closest to. Tim came early to talk a little bit. Aaron stayed late. We really had a good time together. I showed Aaron the crops and the new alfalfa. We drove around with my pickup as it was so wet and almost got stuck in the field. On the way home, I let him drive, and Mary (neighbor) stopped us on the road. She said, "You're a stranger!" so I introduced her, but it was a little awkward. I called Mary later on and told her you can't get away with a thing in this neighborhood! We had a good laugh. I gave Aaron the pictures I had taken at his daughter's graduation party. He was very happy with them.

June 9, 2003

I went to work today and wanted to stop at the grave again on the way home. It was raining by then, and so I drove by but when I looked down the oil road to the church. The sun was brightly shining just at the end of it. I turned around and went back. I put the Ag-Source jacket on again and walked over to the grave in the light rain. I cried and cried. I knew that I had to say goodbye to Merl if I would ever be able to open up my heart to someone else. I told Merl I love him and I will always love him, but I am just so lonely. The tears just poured out of me like the rain that got heavier as I talked. At least this time I took along a paper towel to blow my nose! I pulled up the flowers from Memorial Day. There was thunder and lightning all around me by now, and I wasn't a bit afraid. Finally, I knew I had been there long enough, and I walked to the car. As I was leaving, I looked back at the gravesite one more time, and a beautiful rainbow, a full half (not a quarter) rainbow, was shining so beautiful in the east. I knew it was a sign of hope for me. Maybe there would be someone to share life with here on earth after all.

June 23, 2003

Brad and Des got engaged last night. They are so happy. Brad seems older now, more mature. I am happy for them. Des will be good for Brad. She makes him laugh, and she brings out the best in him. I will miss Brad when he is married. It has been so wonderful to have him living here with me when I go through all of this. But his life has to go on too.

Collette had decided to be baptized at the SunPrairie Baptist Church. She felt it was the right thing to do. When she and Merl had started attending that church, she had asked the pastor if they would bury her if she was not a member. He said yes, not knowing that Merl had only a few short years left. The night before the baptism, Collette took a walk on the road. She asked God to forgive her of her sins. She knew that we are all sinners and to take this step of baptism is huge. When she looked up after praying that God would forgive her, she saw a beautiful rainbow, the half rainbow again. It was beautiful with bright colors. Then she realized that there were no clouds and no rain anywhere. She knew that this was a sign that God was pleased and she was forgiven. The next day, she was baptized at the church. When she told Aaron about it, he said that maybe she was the only one who could see the rainbow.

June 28, 2003

Tonight both Mike and Brad got fired from their job at the angus ranch. The ranch manager called me and told me. I told him it is another blow for the Schocks. How many blows are we supposed to take before we can't get up again? Brad felt he was fired because of his friendship with the ranch manager's daughter. Mike just plain knew too much, and the head boss was always asking him instead of the ranch manager. The kids were all here until 9:00 p.m., talking about it and trying to figure out what to do next. When they all left, I changed clothes and drove down to Aaron. When I got there, the house was dark, and his little white car was gone. I just sat there and cried. Then I saw a light come up from the basement, and Aaron opened the door. I ran up to him and held him and cried. He didn't have a shirt on, and he was wet from sweat, but I didn't care. I told him what had happened. We sat down and talked. He said the boys can't work for someone like that. They will find another job that is better than that one.

He let me talk, and he calmed me down. He didn't have lights because of the storm, but later they came back on, and the house cooled down again. We talked about so many things tonight. I had framed a picture that his wife had drawn of him when he was twenty years old. It was a really cool picture. Earlier, I had showed it to my sister Pat. She said she loved the picture of Merl. I said it's not Merl. But she was sure that it was. I didn't really see the resemblance to Merl the way she did until after she said it. At Aaron's farm, I had it in my car, and I went out to get it. Aaron loved the way I had framed it, and we hung it up in his living room. I told him I was so thankful to April for making that picture. It tells me a lot about him. Of course, he wanted to know what. So I told him that it says he has a kind heart, gentle spirit, and a beautiful soul. I also told him that I am his mission. He told me the story of how his dad met his baseball hero and how that was not luck; it was divine intervention. I said him being home tonight was not luck either; it was also divine intervention. He gave me a special look. He said he would always be here for me. On the way home from his place, I heard Shania Twain's "Forever and Always" I wonder if God is telling me something!

July 1, 2003

Today I got fired! It's the first time in my life I got fired from a job. It's the third Schock to lose a job in four days. This is unbelievable! They really didn't have a reason for firing me. They said I didn't learn the technical part. But I learned what they taught me at the desk, and they didn't spend any time teaching me the optical part. I did not expect this at all. They gave me the money they owed me and said I would not have to go back. I'm done. I came home and told Brad, but he had to leave within a few minutes to go to a meeting. Jenni was not home, as she was at camp. I didn't know how I would tell her this anyway without her becoming so stressed again. I was alone again and had no one to talk to. I tried to figure it out. What went wrong? I know I didn't care much for the job, but I was hoping that didn't come through when I was at work. And they knew when they hired me that I was still in a lot of grief. I called a few people, but no one was home. Finally, at 9:00 p.m. I couldn't stand being alone anymore, so I went see Aaron. I needed him to comfort me. But he was in no frame of mind to be comforting. He was looking for a tire for his tractor in the mosquito-infested trees. He couldn't even stop for a little bit. He didn't have any time for me. I waited around for him awhile but felt I was just in his way. Finally, I got in the car to leave. He said, "Now, I suppose you will be mad at me." I told him I just needed someone to talk to tonight. My pastor was gone on vacation, and my sisters were not home. I didn't have anyone

else to talk to. He told me I would get another
job. He said he felt awful when his girls moved
out. I asked him why he didn't talk to me about
it. He didn't have an answer for me, and then
he started working on his tire. I drove home,
wondering what happened. He was so comfort-
ing and so good to me just a few days ago. Now
when the rest of my world came crashing down,
he was not there for me. It was already almost
dark. He couldn't work much longer, anyway. I
just don't understand.

The next few days were quite depressing for Collette. She tried to figure out what kind of a job to look for. The people at the eye place had said they would give her a good recommendation. But at this point, there wasn't much comfort in that. She went to talk to her pastor and some friends who gave her a boost of confidence again. A couple of days later, she was invited to a birthday party in Mitchell for one of the guys in the grief group. So she went to Mitchell for groceries and stopped by for a while. They met in a bar for supper.

July 3, 2003

Tonight I met a few people from the group
to celebrate John's birthday. We had a pretty good
time, and it got my mind off my problems for
a while. About 11:00 p.m., one of the women
called Aaron and asked him if he was still com-
ing. He said yes. But then most of the people had
to leave, and even John said he had to leave. So
I was left alone there, waiting for Aaron. He

got there a few minutes after everyone else left. He said his tractor broke down, and that's why he was so late. We talked in the bar until they closed it, and then we sat on the street until 2:30 just talking. He said he didn't get the tire fixed anyway. He seemed pretty sheepish. We had good talk tonight. I told him that the most important thing right now is for me to find another job. He said, "No, the most important thing is your personal relationship with Christ." He often had helped me put things in perspective with this one sentence. I asked him if he told April that he loved her. He said he did. We talked about his girls, and my kids, and farming. It was great. I got home tonight later than my kids do—3:00 a.m.

July 4, 2003

Today I feel like I have been freed from bondage. It feels good to not ever have to go back to that job. I didn't like it anyway. I always had the feeling that I would not be there for a very long period of time, but I didn't expect only six months. But there must be something else. Something better is waiting for me. I just have to be patient and ask God what to do.

July 8, 2003

There are two jobs now that I could do. One is to write for a local newspaper. The other was a suggestion from one of the women in the grief group, that I clean houses for people. I really like that idea. I could set my hours, my own pay. I am quite particular about cleaning house. I always have been. If I could work for people who can afford to have that service done, it might work. Brad is exploring custom feeding Holstein heifer calves. It might work, but it is taking quite a chance financially. Then, too, I really don't feel like we have the facilities to do such a thing. Plus it is so time-consuming. He is checking into it.

July 10, 2003

I applied for a few jobs in Mitchell but feel like I don't have a chance. I think I am ready to try the maid. *Des knew someone who did cleaning in SF, and so I called her, and she was very helpful and also encouraging. Today, I made up a flyer with information about my* maid *service. I took it to Mitchell and left it at the hospice dept. in the hospital. Rose said it was a good service, and she might know someone. Also went to Job Service and left a flyer there too. I guess now we just wait.*

July 13, 2003

I went to church today. Don was the usher, and he took my hand to shake it and held it a little bit too long. After church, he came over and talked to me awhile. He said he noticed I lost weight and I look very nice. I wanted to stay about three feet away from him. I felt like he wanted to reach out and grab me. He is really a sweet guy, but I don't want a divorced man.

July 17, 2003

Tonight Aaron called me at 11:00 p.m. He asked me to go along to MN to a ball game. Tim is going and maybe two others from the group. I don't care much for baseball, but I could sure use an outing like that. I hope I can go. It's this weekend, so will have to make arrangements to be gone.

July 18, 2003

Tonight I went to church. I sat in the sanctuary and talked to God. I told Him that I will miss being there on Sunday—to please take care of all of us, and if there would be any chance for happiness for me, please let it happen. Then I went out to Merl's grave, and I talked to him and cried. I told him again I will always love him, no matter what. I know he didn't tell me it was okay to love again because it was just too hard.

July 21, 2003

I went to Aaron's place, and Tim came, and we left for Minneapolis to the Twins game. Aaron drove. It was a lot of fun to visit with the guys. We talked nonstop all the way up there, a lot of it was about farming. When we got to

Minneapolis, we went around and around and couldn't get to the dome. Finally, Aaron yelled out the window and asked a guy where the Metrodome is. He said he was going there, and we just followed him. There we met Aaron's sister and husband and their friends. They gave us tickets to get into the game. We met Aaron's nephew who was a player for the Twins. I told him he is as handsome as his uncle. He gave me the biggest smile! Also saw Aaron's dad who had driven up by himself. He gave me a big hug when he saw me, and we talked awhile. The game was great, and then we went to find a motel. We were able to get rooms in the same motel as Aaron's family. Aaron and Tim had one room, and I had another one. They were the last rooms available in the motel. Tim and Aaron and I talked a long time after the rest had gone to bed. It was a great day.

July 22, 2003

Sunday, we rode the shuttle bus to the Metrodome and met another one of the grief group and her children. Aaron's sister gave us tickets to sit with them again, so we had premium seats. It was another great game, and we all had fun. When it was over, Tim decided to ride along home with Aaron's dad, since he was driving home alone. So that left Aaron and me to drive home together. We had a great time, talking all the way. We followed closely so that we could have supper together with his dad and Tim at Fairbault. After that we lost them, as his dad drove quite fast. We enjoyed the ride and played CDs in the car and never ran out of things to talk about. We were deep in discussion. After what seemed like a long time, I noticed the road signs had names of towns in Iowa. We had missed the interstate exit to go back to SD and had gone south into Iowa about seventy-five miles. Aaron felt bad, but I just laughed and laughed. We pulled over and got out a road map, but neither one of us could read it very good without bifocals. Two blind old people took a trip into Iowa! I told Aaron that God wanted us to have a good visit, and maybe an adventure. We had to find a station that still sold gas, and I drove from there. Aaron fell asleep when I started to drive. By the time we got into South Dakota, I was in my home territory and took back roads to save time. But I got lost in the town of Parker and couldn't figure out how to get out of town. Finally, I started laughing again. Aaron heard me and woke up. I told him, "I am so tired. I am hysterical, but don't worry. Just go back to sleep." So I found my way out of town, and we drove into his yard at 2:45 a.m. I told him it was a fantastic time, one I will never forget, gave him a big hug, and went home.

The next few days were busy with farm decisions. They discovered that the corn in the bins was moldy and buggy. They needed to sell it, even though they would take dockage for it. She made some contracts for the corn that was growing in the field. That made her feel good again, as it was something she did all by herself. Because she had a job in town, she had lost about $6,000 by not watching the markets and selling the corn earlier. She remembered that Aaron had said she would be okay if she just stayed home. But she had felt that there would not be enough money without a job. They moved cattle that week, and the neighbors helped, and all the kids were there. They had pizza afterward and had a good time together.

When Saturday came, she loaded up the lawnmower and cleaning supplies and headed for Aaron's house. She had promised him to help clean up his yard and house for a grief group party there on Sunday afternoon. At first, it was good time together, and they had fun while they worked, but later on, he said that he works better alone. Collette was so hurt. He left then and ran an errand into town. When he came back, they had some honest conversation. He asked her, "Have I ever given you any indication that I liked you more than the rest of the people in the group?"

"No, but I wish you would," replied Collette with a twinkle in her eye and a smile.

He sat down on the basement steps, and they talked. He said, "I need time. I'm not ready for anything yet, and I can't be rushed."

"I'm not trying to push you into anything. I just need to talk to you because I know you understand. You and April farmed like Merl, and I did, and I need some help now to keep the farm and the kids going. We connect in a spiritual way, and I know God sent you to help me. I am your mission, and I hope I can help you too," Collette said.

Aaron said, "Sometimes I just want to move far away."

Collette said, "That is just running away. You can't run away from your problems. They follow you. Talk to me and let me help you through some of your grief too." He didn't say any more, so she gathered her things together to leave. She said, "I care about you, Aaron."

He said, "I care about you too," as he held her hands and smiled that special smile. He gave her a big hug before she left.

The next day, she got ready to go to Aaron's party. She wondered what he would be like today. When she got there, he was happy to see her, and they had a good time with the people who came from the group. Aaron's parents were there and also some of his friends. The bathroom was upstairs in the house, and when Collette went up there to use it in the course of the day, she noticed pictures in the stairway. She instantly knew that she had seen that hallway before with those pictures. It was the same feeling she had when she met Aaron's dad for the first time. She was so sure she had met him before. Later in the afternoon, people started leaving. Collette was the last one to leave. She told Aaron, "I'm glad we had a chance to talk honestly yesterday."

He said, "I am too."

"I don't ever want to lose you as a friend. Will you call me?"

He said, "Yes, but you can call me too."

The next days and weeks found Collette starting to do things for others. Pastor had stopped and asked if she would want to go and see a man from church who was near death from cancer. She said she would go. Tim had e-mailed her and said he would say a prayer for her as she did this. She really appreciated his support. When Collette was there, she talked about how she had felt God's presence in the room when Merl died. How there was no fear anywhere, only peace. She also asked him to tell Merl when he sees him that she still loves him very much and misses him. She felt good about going there. He passed away a few days later.

Brad had bought a 6620 turbo combine and was looking for a bean head. So Brad and Collette went to Yankton to look at one. They decided it was a piece of junk and didn't buy it. When they got into the car to go home, the radio just started to play "Copperhead Road" by Steve Earle. This was one of Merl's favorite songs from the late 1980s, and they seldom played it anymore. Collette told Brad that Dad must be telling us we did the right thing. Brad agreed. Collette told Brad, "I think Dad can communicate with us through the radio. He seems to have done this from the beginning. I also think he is in charge of rainbows."

The next few days, Brad and Collette made a trip into Iowa to go to a school about feeding Holstein calves. They enjoyed the time away from home and learned a little bit along the way.

When they came home from Iowa, Jenni went with Collette to see Jeff's grandma. She also had cancer and was near the end. Collette tried to reassure her too that it would be wonderful when she sees Jesus. She passed away that night. Collette was so glad she could go and see her one last time.

The days of August were hard to go through. August 18 would have been their thirtieth wedding anniversary. Collette planned a weekend trip to Lake Okoboji and took the whole family. Jeff did not go along because his grandma had died, and the funeral was during the time they were gone. Collette told Jenni that maybe the timing was so that she would not have to go through that funeral. Jeff's grandma was someone she knew so well who also died from cancer, and it would have been hard for her. Jenni felt bad to miss it. The weekend getaway was good for all of them. They went on a dinner cruise and spent time in the lake and also the pool. They did some shopping and ended up renting jet skis. Collette was so sad through it all, but she did her best to hide it. She realized that her children were young, and they didn't want to be sad all the time. They wanted to be able to move on with life.

When they got home from the weekend trip, there were two job offers on the answering machine. One was a job at another eye clinic, that Collette was not interested in. The other was a young woman's voice who wanted to know if Collette would clean her mother's house. Her mother was dying of cancer, and it was important to her to have someone take care of her house when she was gone. Collette wrote in her journal,

August 20, 2003

Is this what God wants me to do? Comfort the dying and those left behind? I just don't know if I can do it. I don't say the right things anyway. Isn't getting Merl to heaven enough? Maybe He took him so I could do this. I want to talk to Aaron about it. I am so confused, and he is the only one I can talk to about God. He won't think I am crazy. My family and friends already think I am not sane. But Aaron knows that I saw rainbows. He believes I am the only one who could see them. But I don't want to bother him. I feel like I talk to him and go see him too often when he really doesn't want me there. Doesn't he know that this is his mission too?

The next morning, Collette wrestled with it but finally picked up the phone to call Aaron. He was happy to hear from her, and they talked awhile. She asked if she could come down. He answered that it was okay and seemed to be all right with it. So she stopped at the elevator on the way and took some apple bars she had made for him. He was happy to see her, and they had a lot to talk about. She said he could buy her combine if he wanted it. He said he would take her up on that. She told him about the housecleaning job and talking to people who are dying. He thought it was God telling her to do it. He also said she would be better off setting her own hours. When she left, he told her she was getting her life together. On the way home, she stopped to see his parents. She took them a jar of pickles and a jar of jam she had made. They were so easy to visit with, and she stayed longer than she had intended. They were so kind and interesting. At the end of the day, she picked up her Bible, and it came to this page, Jeremiah 29:11: "For I know the plans I have for you, plans to prosper you and not to harm you, plans to give you hope and a future."

The next Saturday, Collette went to talk to the Mader family. She met Sharon. Collette told Sharon she is going to a better place. Sharon said, "Well, we hope so."

Collette said, "No, I know so! I could feel it when Merl took his last breath, there was no fear in the room, only peace. I don't know how it all works. Was it Merl I felt in the room with me after he died, or was it God Himself? But I know Merl has peace, the peace that comes from God when we ask for forgiveness of sins and believe in God."

Collette promised Sharon that she would be there to help Luke keep the house clean for as long as she possibly could. Collette could see that it helped Sharon to let go of life here, just a little bit.

At this same time, Collette was reading a book that Aaron had recommended to her *Embraced by the Light*, by Betty J. Eadie. It said that we have free will, but if we ask for help from

God by prayer, He will answer us. There were things in the book that Collette already knew, like the fact that if you let them, negative thoughts can make you ill. That fear is the opposite of love. That God is totally love. He is not the angry, feared God that some make Him out to be. Aaron had given the book to Collette some time ago, but she had not wanted to read it. Now she could not put it down.

The days that lead up to August 30 were busy days. They were cutting haylage. The boy's cousin Brian came up to help. Mike's cattle broke out, and they all had to go over and get them back in. At least it was a distraction to facing the fact that a year had passed without Merl in her life. She wrote in her journal,

August 30, 2003

Today is it. Today is a whole year that Merl is gone. I remember it all too well. I didn't sleep very well that night, and when I finally did fall asleep, I couldn't wake up, so I rushed to take a shower. Then I came out and touched his cheek and told him, "I am here now." Soon after that, he quit breathing. Right after that, Jenni came out of the shower, and she knew by the look on my face that he was gone. Today I tried to keep busy. But it was hard to keep busy. Every time I sat down for just a minute, I thought of him. I love him so very much, no matter what. I feel like I have passed over a mountain today. What the other side will be like, only God knows. I wish He would send me an e-mail. I still pray there will be some happiness in my life. I don't

know how I can be of any use to God if I am so
unhappy and lonely.

The next weekend, Collette and the grief group went camping in Chamberlain on the river. Collette borrowed a tent from Mike and Joann, took some food and a few supplies, and headed over there. It was good weather that weekend, and they had good time together. A large group attended, as some of the people had children that were there also. There were also two boats to give rides and pull tubes for the kids. They had camp-fires and good food and fun. But they also talked about problems they were having with their children and life in general. Collette came home early on Sunday to spend some time with Jenni before she went back to school again.

Collette started going to Luke every week to clean house for him. Sharon had passed away, and Collette attended the prayer service for her. She knew how deep their loss was and how hard the next year would be for Luke. When she came to clean, she tried to visit with Luke to see how he was doing. He was tall, good-looking, and had deep-brown eyes. He was a farmer and a few years older than she was. He told her how Sharon had fought the cancer. She was so brave, but she just couldn't beat it. Collette knew to let him talk about it. She told him that she believed that we are put on this earth to help each other and she would be there to help him work through his grief. After a while, he went outside to do some work on the farm. She tried to clean everything the best she could. She sat down in the living room for a minute to rest. She noticed a ceiling fan and thought maybe she should clean it. She worked on some other rooms, came back through the living room, and looked at the fan again. But there was the kitchen to do yet, and she was running out of time. Later, she felt she must clean that fan yet before she leaves, so she got a ladder and climbed up there to clean it. When she got done, she said, "Okay, Sharon, are you happy now!" It felt as though Sharon was there, telling her that the ceiling fan needed cleaning!

September 16, 2003

Today is two years ago that April died. I called Aaron, but he didn't answer, so I got in the car and drove down there. He said he was sleeping so hard, he didn't hear the phone. I'm sure he didn't sleep much last night. I told him God sent me instead of an angel today and that I would go with him to April's grave. But he wouldn't go. He said if he goes, he will be sad all day. I didn't force it on him. I felt he had to do what he felt was best. Today he didn't have any beans to grind to make coffee, but we sat down to visit, anyway. On my way home, I put the silk rose I had brought on April's grave. It made me cry to see there was just a marker there instead of a tombstone after two years. I told her that he is a good man and he misses her so very much."

Now it was time to cut corn silage. It seemed like the cows always broke out as the fences on the farm were not very good. Collette could run pretty fast by now, as she had gone from a size 18 to a size 10. Her friends told her she was an inspiration and that she looked about sixteen years old. She was so glad to lose the weight and get off medication for type 2 diabetes. Her drive to lose the weight had come from the knowledge that she is the only parent left and she has to be in good health for a long time. Her only regret was that Merl was not here to see it. He would have been very proud of her.

The last days of September were very hard for Luke. He tried very hard to not let Collette see how sad he was. She invited him to go with her to the grief group meetings. At first, he said he would think about it, but then he declined. So she didn't push it, knowing he needed time to process all his grief. She offered to cook some meals for him, but he declined that also. She thought he is trying so hard to go on alone. But they still had good conversation on the days she cleaned.

Tim was still calling Collette and had wanted to take her to Italy with him. He had some family there that he wanted her to meet. She politely said she could not go with him. Another man kept calling her to ask her out, but Collette just wanted to hear from Aaron. Finally he called, and he came up the next day. Collette had told him that he could buy her combine. It was already the end of September, and she knew that he needed time to get it ready for the field. Brad had purchased a 6620 turbo combine, and she didn't have a place to store another combine. It was sad to let the combine go that Merl and her had used for eleven years. But she knew he would appreciate having it, and he really needed it. He drove it down the road toward his farm, and Collette followed with his car. When they got close to Emery, he asked if she would drive the combine around the town while he went into the town for supplies. She said she would love to. As he watched her drive the combine away, she realized that maybe he just wanted to see if she could really drive it, like she had said! When they got to his farm, John was there with a friend, and they had been hunting geese.

They visited awhile, and then Aaron and Collette drove back to Collette's place with Aaron's pickup. Aaron had just bought a used pickup from another person in the group. When they got to Collette's place, Brad helped Aaron put the chopper from the combine on the back of his pickup. Collette watched him leave and wondered if he would ever realize that she could be good for him.

The next week, there was a grief group meeting at Platte. Collette drove out there herself. During the course of the day, Collette couldn't help herself. She cried as she told them that she was not a part of the farming anymore. The girls helped her boys farm, and she was an outsider. She lost her husband, best friend, and whole way of life. Aaron just listened and didn't say a word. But later he said he had a little bit to do yet before combining, but then he would call her, and she could run the combine if she wanted while he hauled the loads. She told him she would love to!

The first part of October, Mike and Brad started combining beans and were done about the seventh. The beans averaged 23 bushels per acre. They had looked so good early in the year, and then it just never rained. Collette said she thought Merl would make it rain. She decided he must be in charge of rainbows, not rain. When their bean harvest was done, she waited for Aaron to call like he said he would. Finally, she couldn't take it and stopped there one day on her way home from Mitchell. He was working on the combine and had not got it going yet. She knew it would take some time for him to get everything ready to go, and that's why she had wanted him to get the combine earlier. He told her he meant it when he said he was going to call her. They talked while he worked on it, and he got it done that night. For the next two days, Collette helped him with bean harvest. They worked good together and had a good time doing it. Aaron was very appreciative of her help. It just felt right to both of them.

That weekend, Collette went to a women's retreat with a good friend from church. The speaker was inspiring, and at the end of her speech, she had music playing for a time of reflection. Collette put her head toward heaven and closed her eyes. She let God put pictures in her mind. She saw Merl lying in the bed just before he died. She saw the rainbow at the grave site and the rainbow on the night before her baptism when there was no rain and no clouds. She saw Aaron coming up from the basement with the flashlight the night the boys got fired. Tears rolled down her cheeks as she realized that through everything that happened, God's love surrounded her. She knew that God was with her and He would continue to take care of her.

The next weeks found Collette helping the boys combine corn. Young people think you should work all night long, at least that's what Brad thought. Collette found herself running the grain cart (two wagons hooked together) unloading in the dark till almost midnight. But she did enjoy being out there with the boys. Jenni came home on the weekends to help too. The sun set was so beautiful those nights, with just a wisp of clouds. The air was crisp and felt good. She had lost more weight, and so clothes just hung loose on her. On the weekends, she worked for a bed and breakfast that had hunters. They were good people to work for, and she enjoyed it, but it kept her very busy. She wondered if Aaron ever got his beans done. She knew that he was extremely busy too. One Sunday night, she called him, and he answered the phone. He said the starter was out on the combine and he had not got it fixed yet. His truck also needed repair, his daughter needed help to move, and the hunters had taken a lot of his time. She said she would come back to help him whenever she could. The weather was changing by this time. It was almost the end of October. Snow was predicted, and it seemed to rain a small amount often. Collette and the boys combined corn until 2:00 a.m. a few nights in a row and managed to get done.

Then Collette went back down to help Aaron. Collette took along one of her wagons to make Aaron's harvest go faster. He had more breakdowns, and it took another full day to get a combine going. They did some combining, but then it snowed. It felt so good to both of them to be able to do some combining/farming together, as Aaron missed April's help too.

Collette was getting more maid jobs. It was almost full-time by now. She was working all the time either as the maid or farming. But work was what she did, and she didn't mind it. It helped in the grieving process. She still thought of Merl at every turn. She loved harvest with Merl and helping Aaron reminded her of some good times with Merl.

From time to time, she went to Merl's grave to talk to him. She wrote in her journal,

> November 18, 2003
>
> *There is so much going on these days. I am working more and more hours. But I think it is good. I went up to Merl's grave tonight. I cried and cried. I didn't even know what for this time. It just felt like it was time to go up there and cry. I guess I cried for farming. Brad will farm the rented ground next year. I am still so worried about money and how it will all come out. We don't worship money or want to get rich.*

We only want to be able to pay bills and make payments. After a while, I knew that I should go, but I wanted to stay. It is always that way. Finally, I said, "God's plan is perfect. I will see you again." And I walked away. I went into the sanctuary and sat there a while. I felt God's presence there and felt God's arms around me, comforting me. I know I have a lot on my plate. I pray that I will be able to support myself and keep my family going. But I know I have God helping me through each day, and there is no way I can give up as long as I have Him. I just pray that God will lead us on the path He has for us. You know, God, an e-mail would be so helpful!

Collette always spent time with Luke when she cleaned, trying to get him to talk about his feeling of grief for Sharon. Sometimes, he was just too sad to talk. She knew he was in such pain. Sharon had taken care of so many things for him, keeping the house spotless, meals prepared, and bookwork done. Now he had to do these things for himself. He was always very appreciative of her housecleaning. She knew it made him a little sad to come into a clean house and not have Sharon there just finishing up. Every week, she found out a little bit more about his life with Sharon.

All through November, the Schock family was still trying to get things done before winter set in. One Saturday, they spent the day hauling in cornstalk bales until way after dark. Brad loaded the bales, Mike unloaded, and Jenni and Collette hauled them home. The next day, they woke up to snow, so they were very glad they had worked so hard. There were a lot of late nights in the fall, as they all had jobs or school to do during the day. Brad did subbing at the local school and also worked part-time at a vet, and Collette was doing more and more *maid* work. It seemed like they were always chasing cows that got out. The problem was that the fences were still for milk cows. Milk cows will stay in with just one wire that is electric. They know they will be fed enough and are tamer, because they go into the barn. The stock cows are wilder, and the fences they had at this time were not good enough to hold them. This proved to be a huge challenge for them, as they spent so much time away from home.

The grief group met in Sioux Falls to go Christmas shopping again this year, but Collette did not go with them. Collette had not heard from Aaron for a while, so she called him one night. She told him she had lots of leftovers from the weekend, and he could come for supper if he wanted. He politely refused. He was getting ready to go to his nephew's wedding out of state and would be gone a few days. He had already figured out that Collette was a good cook and said he would have liked to come.

Collette tried to deal with life each day. Her car was still giving her grief and was always in the shop. It was a constant expense. When Aaron got back from the trip, he said he would bring Collette's wagon back, and she asked him if he would tow her car to the auto shop. So he came and they had another good day together. He told her about the wedding and his trip. And they had deep conversation again. Aaron asked her, "Do you think Merl and April were supposed to die now, together?"

"I don't know. I don't understand any of it. But I know God always has a plan," she replied.

She asked him, "Did April have faults?"

He said no immediately but later said that maybe she did.

Collette said, "I think it is important to remember our loved ones the way they truly were. We should not dwell on the bad things, but remember, they were human and only did the best they could. Merl knew he had faults, but he also knew that I loved him, anyway. And I am so glad he loved me despite my faults too."

They made plans for him to come back and cut some trees for firewood. When he left, Collette remembered a passage in the Bible. First Corinthians 7:39 says, "A woman is bound to her husband as long as he lives. But if her husband dies, she is free to marry anyone she wishes, but he must belong to the Lord." She thought Aaron belongs to the Lord; of that, she was certain.

Now it was December, and Christmas was around the corner again. Collette did not look forward to another Christmas without Merl. But she knew she had been through it last year, and she would survive it again this year. One day, in the mail, she received a strange envelope. It was a plain long envelope with no return address. Her name was typed on the front. When she opened it, she just prayed that it would not be another bill. To her surprise, it was a blank piece of paper with two one-hundred-dollar bills. To think that someone thought of her in need meant so much to her. She just cried when she saw it. She had always wanted to be on the giving end and not the getting end. She wondered who could have sent it. She had a family who was so supportive, and so many good friends, the college friends, friends from church, and her best friend from the grief group. No one took credit for it, of course. It meant so much to Collette. She finally got a hold of herself enough to buy some Christmas presents. Until that time, she had been too depressed to even try.

Some people from the grief group were planning on going on a cruise. Collette really contemplated going. She had never been on a trip like that before and now didn't have anyone to go with on any trips. She kept thinking maybe she could go. She talked it over with her friends. They were quite encouraging. But her best friend of the group could not go. After much debate, she finally realized that she needed a better car much more than she needed a cruise.

A couple of days before Christmas, Collette went to Aaron's place. He helped her make a gag gift for Brad and Des for Christmas. He also fixed the coffee grinder that had belonged to her parents. She was thrilled to have it in working order again. She gave him a picture of herself. She had lost almost sixty pounds by now. She also had blown up a picture of him with the combine he bought from her. He really liked the pictures. He asked about Luke. She told him that he is very nice but in a lot of grief. They had a good evening together.

On Christmas Eve, Jenni went with Collette to SunPrairie's candlelight service. Later, Collette went to Trinity Church's Christmas service and visited with so many people she had not seen in a while. It truly felt like Christmas, the celebration of Christ's birth. She came home to an empty house and had a little supper. She felt quite alone but kept her spirits up by listening to Christmas carols on the radio.

On Christmas Day, all the kids were there for supper. She made potato roll, a favorite from the Schock side of the family. They opened presents and stayed up until 1:00 a.m. She missed Merl very much but realized that she must try to be happy for the sake of her family.

On New Year's Eve, her car didn't work again, but Brad let her use his car to drive to friends, LaVetta and Gayle. Mike and Joann, Brad and Des, and Jenni and Jeff came too. Gayle told lots of funny stories, and they all had a good time together. Collette wondered what the next year would bring. Brad would get married and move out of her house. She knew that would be a big change, but she was happy for him. She felt she just had to give it all to God and let Him lead her.

Brad and Desiree driving Brad's JD 6620 turbo combine
from wedding to reception in Lennox, SD

Chapter 6

2004 – All You Need To Do Is Ask

The new year started with Collette's car still not working. She just didn't know what to do with it. She took it back up to the repair shop in Howard for them to figure out what was wrong. They drove it seventy-five miles, and it worked just fine.

Collette went back to work at Luke. She was all ready to confess that she had caught the tree skirt in the vacuum cleaner just before Christmas, but he already knew about it. She had made a new one for him. She thanked him for the fifty dollars for Christmas. He teased her and said, "Was it 50? Honey, I thought it was a 5."

She thought he probably called everyone Honey. He seemed better today.

The next Monday, Brad and Des and Collette went to Brooking to a meeting about Holstein bull calves. Brad came away from that meeting and decided on his own that it was not something that would work. Collette was so relieved as she had reservations about it from the beginning.

Collette thought about the night that she had been at Aaron's house before Christmas. He had walked out of the house in front of her, as if to say, "This is long enough. You go home now." She was hurt by that but realized that he probably was tired of her being around. She knew that she needed to not call and wait for him to call her instead. One night, she read the book of Job. She wrote in the journal.

> January 6, 2004
>
> *I just finished reading the book of Job. I don't know that there were any answers there or not. I guess suffering is part of life here on earth. We are not to question God. After all, He is the Almighty. He knows all. It's just that we don't know anything. Someday we will know too, and until then we are to trust God to take care of us and lead us in life every day. I know that I have to totally give everything over to God. It is so easy to want to take life back and run it ourselves. I know I can't do that. I have to give everything over to God. And then He will give back to me what I need, now and always."*

Des had found a red 1997 Oldsmobile for Collette in a car lot. She showed it to Collette, and they were so excited about it. Collette loved the color red. She liked her 1992 Oldsmobile. It's just that it was giving her so much trouble right now. The car would shut off in the middle of driving sixty miles per hour. She would coast to the side and sit there, and then it would not start. She had taken it in for repair several times, but they couldn't find anything wrong with it. It would start up just fine and run perfectly for them. Des stopped in at the dealership and asked questions about the red car. They said it belonged to a man from Sioux Falls whose wife had died. It was her car, and he didn't want to look at it any longer. When Collette found that out, it stopped her in her tracks. She wanted to go and look at it. So on Saturday, Mike and Brad went along with Collette and Desiree met them there. Collette drove it, and she loved it. As she came back to the dealer, she thought there weren't even any dents to complain about, as the price they asked was too high. But when she got back, the salesman got into the car one last time before they went inside to talk price. He noticed the "service engine soon" light came on. The guys took it in the shop but could not find anything wrong with it. Collette knew that at a certain mileage, a car would automatically put that light on. She was not the least bit worried about it. However, it was something to complain about and get the price lower. Brad was really good at negotiating, and she got the car for a price she could afford. Mike and Brad drove her 1992 on the way home, and she drove the 1997. She couldn't believe she got it. It was what she had always wanted. The salesman had said that the woman had driven this car to a picnic area and committed suicide. Collette felt so bad for her husband. On the way home, the lights flashed four times, stopped for a minute, and then started again. She wasn't concerned at first, thinking maybe she had accidently hit a button. After she got home, the lights continued to flash. It flashed whether the car was running or not. She called back to the dealership, but the mechanics had no idea what button she might have pushed to make such a thing happen. She would have to wait till Monday to come back in, and they would look at it. She called Mike to come over and look at it. They looked all over but could not figure out what was wrong. So she parked it behind the house in case it started on fire in the night. At least it would not burn down the garage. That night, she did not sleep very well and looked out the window a few times at the car. It was still flashing the lights. She was just sure the battery would be dead in the morning. But the next morning, the car started right up. She went back into the house and sat down to think. The only person who could possibly figure this out would be the former owner. At the dealership, Collette had asked for the name of the former owner, but that was illegal to give out. However, since she bought it, she saw the title, and remembered the name that was on it. She called him. She explained the situation and asked if there was anything he could think of that she could do to stop the flashing. At first he was quite sympathetic, but didn't know of anything. Finally, she asked him why he sold the car. He said it was his wife's car and she had died. Actually, she had committed suicide and he didn't want to see the car setting there anymore because it reminded him. At first Collette didn't know what to say. Finally, she said she does know what it feels like to lose someone you love so very much. She told him that her husband had died of cancer about a year ago. Then he said he would look at the car if she wanted to drive it back into Sioux Falls. She said she would be happy to if there was any chance he could fix it. As Collette drove into Sioux Falls, she prayed that God would tell her what to say to comfort him. When she met him, she knew immediately that he was extremely depressed. Usually, she had no problem getting someone to talk, but he was a real challenge. Finally, she started talking about the experience of losing Merl. He listened intently, and then he started to open up too. She asked if he had friends he could talk to. He said not really and that mostly he was alone. She encouraged him to join a grief group. She asked him about his wife, got him to talk, and just listened. It was what he needed most. She told him that God loves him and is with him through it all. He fixed the car. He unhooked some wires under the dash, and when he hooked them back up, the car was fine. He had hooked up a remote car starter and gave her the remote. He had kept the remote in his garage when he sold the car. When she left, he seemed much better.

The next day, she called the salesman back. She asked him if he believed in God. He said he did. She told him that God worked through him to sell her the car. She had met the former owner, and he was going through such a tough time. She was able to talk to him about his grief because she was experiencing the loss of a loved one too.

The next grief group gathering was in Mitchell. She talked briefly to Aaron, and he wanted to see her new car. He opened the hood and checked it all out. He said the remote start was worth about $500. She was so surprised that it cost that much and so happy that this man would give it to her. She asked Aaron if he was still going to take her out for supper for helping him harvest. He said they would just have to pick a day to go. So the next Friday, he called her about 4:00 p.m. and asked if she still wanted to go out for supper with him. She said yes, and he came up a couple of hours later to get her. They went to Sioux Falls and talked nonstop all night. They talked about their families and farming and God and faith. He told her that he had not paid his phone bill, and he had to drive into town to pay it so they would put the phone back on and he could call her that night. She was impressed that he would do that for her. She told him that her nephew had researched the cruise. It is an old ship, and there weren't any flights into New Orleans except for two days before the ship left. He said he had already decided not to go. They drove through the machinery lots, and he talked about machinery he planned to buy. He told her again, not to overdue on the maid business as it will be too hard on her. They enjoyed the time together, and when it was over, he held her close, and his eyes twinkled as he said goodnight.

On Friday, she went to Luke again. She was cleaning the light fixture in the kitchen when suddenly it fell off the ceiling. She just held on until he came and rescued her. She told him that she wrecks more than she's worth. He didn't seem to mind and found it quite amusing to see her hanging on to the light like that. But then he found a lot of things amusing. She could see he had a good sense of humor, and she liked that.

Winter in South Dakota can be brutal, and that week, it came back with full force. It was -37 degrees, and then it snowed. Her work was canceled. She lost $180 that week, and one of her customers called and said she cannot afford to keep her. So that meant a loss of $70 per week hereafter. At first, she was sad, as she really liked the customer. But she tried to keep thinking positive, and it didn't take long, and she filled the $70 per week opening with a $90 per week job.

The next week, she went to Luke and knocked over a vase. It didn't break, but again she wondered why she was so clumsy in that house. She figured if she wanted to keep that job, she better not break any more things. He made fun of her that she baked flax muffins. She said she would invite him over sometime and serve him a little flax without him knowing it!

Even though the days were cold, her remote start worked every time, and she was so thankful for a reliable car. She got a large envelope in the mail from the former owner of her red car. He sent her the cd player book and the remote starter book. He also sent a nice little note. It meant a lot to her that he would do that for her. She called him to thank him, and they talked a while. He seemed to be doing better.

February 4, 2004

Today was Merl's birthday, but it wasn't. He isn't here to have a birthday—to be fifty-two. I cleaned all day. You have heard of the singing maid. Well, today I was the crying maid. I miss Merl so very much. I didn't know it would be this hard again. But it doesn't seem to get any easier. I went to Larry's place over my noon hour, but he was too busy to talk to me. Their yard was full of snow, and I almost got stuck in the yard. Brian opened it up so I could get back out. Connie met me for supper. It was so good to have time with my cousin, especially today. I needed Connie to make me laugh, and she did. Late in the evening, Brad told me his experience today. He substituted at the school all day and then helped milk cows at Larry's. He got home after dark, and he still had to feed our cows. He got into the 1086, and the lights didn't work. He knew he needed to fix something on the lights, but he had been gone all day and didn't even have parts. He tried the lights again, and nothing. He got out of the tractor and just didn't know what to do. He needed that tractor to feed, and he couldn't do anything without lights. So he climbed into the cab once more, and he prayed, "God, please let the lights work. I really need the lights to work." He hit

the switch. and the lights came on. I told him,
"Brad, sometimes all you need to do is ask!"

Collette started cleaning at the new job and thought it was a wonderful place to work. It was a very old house that had so much character, yet it was modern and remodeled too. The Tieszens were very generous and really appreciated her. She started working there every week, just like she did for Luke. Not long after she started, she was cleaning in the bathroom, and a frame fell down and broke open. There behind the picture was a twenty-dollar bill. She took it out and put the frame back together. When she was done for the day, she left the money with a note that explained what happened. She told them that she once found money behind a frame that she had bought in a thrift store and thought maybe that was where this frame was from too. Collette knew that the most important thing in business, especially maid business, was to be trustworthy.

Collette had told Aaron that she was taking all her kids out for supper to Sioux Falls one weekend, and he could come too. He was happy to go along to visit with the family. She picked him up, and they met the rest of the family in Sioux Falls. They were lots of fun like always. Mike and Brad were cracking jokes all night, almost embarrassing her. Jenni asked what her mom had broken at Luke recently. So Collette had to explain how she had ripped the tree skirt, light fixture fell down, and the lamp fell over. After supper, they all went to Menards and did some shopping. Collette let Aaron drive her new red car, and the first thing he did was peel out of the parking lot! Aaron agreed to put a carpet in Collette's bedroom for the second half of the money Aaron owed Collette for the combine. Brad said he would probably be around to help too. Aaron and Collette decided to get together the next weekend when the rest would be on the cruise.

February 16, 2004

Tonight I went out to feed the cats in the barn. I was filled with so many wonderful memories of Merl out there. I could see him milking the cows, sitting on the bench and petting the cats, or singing with the radio. I turned around and looked toward the door, and there sat a huge opossum. He was as big as the cats, only fatter, just staring at me with his beady eyes. He didn't budge even though I screamed very loud. The cats just looked at me. They think he is their ugly cousin. I decided he wasn't going to run, so I would have to. I took a run for it and ran right by him to get out the door. When Brad came home, I told him about it. He took the gun, blasted the barn door open, and flicked on the lights. There sat the opossum. Brad shot him, and he ran under a pallet. Brad poked the gun under there and shot him again. This time he got him. When Brad fired the shots in the barn, the cats flew up the walls. They weren't going to hang around to see what happened to their ugly cousin. This is what life is like, living with Jethroe. I'm going to miss that guy!

February 19, 2004

Mike and Joann came over tonight to tell me they are having a baby in September. I don't know how I feel about being a grandma. I guess it makes me sad because Merl is not here to be grandpa. We were supposed to go through all these big things in life together. How can he not be here for this? I still don't understand, and my heart is aching. I'm sure the kids don't understand why I wasn't jumping for joy when they told me. They just don't understand what I am going through and how hard everything is in life now. The world keeps turning when my world stopped.

Aaron and Collette did get together the weekend of the cruise. They had a little supper together, and she brought a video to watch. But Aaron fell asleep in the chair the minute the video started. She watched him sleep almost an hour and then went outside to start the car. When she came in, he woke up. She asked if he would come the next weekend to put the rug in her bedroom. He said he would, and then she left. She thought when she left, "He is such an old man, sometimes!"

The week went by. A man Collette knew kept calling her. He said he was determined to get her to go out with him. She told him she was not interested, but he still called to talk. She knew he was just lonely too. Tim had told Collette that he met a woman on an Internet site. She came to one of the grief meetings, and Collette thought she was very nice. Collette looked up the same website and found a farmer from MO that seemed interesting, but she didn't contact him. At least she knew it was a possibility.

That next Saturday, Brad crawled into Collette's room and said his back hurt. She would have to do the chores. So she did, and Brad went to rest. She knew right away, he would not be available to help Aaron with the rug installation. Aaron came up and then Collette helped him the best she could. She told him that today she would be his "lovely assistant." They worked pretty good together and had a good visit too. They put a new carpet in her bedroom. It was a lot of work, but they got it done. They only had a little bit to finish up after supper, and he left about 9:30, very tired. She slept very good with the smell of new carpet. The sun woke her up, as there were no shades on the windows. The next few days, she got the room back in order. It felt good to have something nice. She knew that Aaron would rather have done the labor for her than pay more money for the combine. It worked out for both of them.

Aaron and Collette started working on building a frame for Aaron's daughter, who was getting married. Collette came up with the idea, and she wanted it to be something that Aaron made for his daughter. She did this without him even knowing that was her intention. He was quite handy with fixing, and she knew he could make it. It was a frame made out of tree branches, with roses and ivy wrapped around the branches. They didn't get to working on it until late at night, so it ended up very late when she got home. The first night, she got home at 3:00 a.m. after working on this project. Brad met her at the door. He said, "This has got to stop—coming home in the middle of the night! You have to be home by midnight."

She asked him, "Are you really upset?"

He said, "No, it's just payback time."

She told him what her plan was and what they were working on. But it was not done yet, so she might have to come home late another night or two!

Sunday, there was another grief group gathering. By this time, these get-togethers were just to keep in touch. There was not as much talk about loss of spouses as there once had been. Several people were dating, and some used the Internet. Tim asked Collette if she had found anyone on the Internet. She said she actually had found someone… for her cousin. She told them that Internet dating was not for her. One of the guys in the group was going to get married to a person who was much younger than he was. He was sure it was the right thing to do, but his friends tried to talk him out of it.

The next week brought more maid work. Collette was always busy. She enjoyed the time at the huge older home. She spent a whole day in that house and often had her little radio with her when she cleaned. She was still listening to songs that made her cry like "I Miss My Friend" by Darol Worley. Collette could relate to the words of the song. She thought how she had lost so much, her husband, father to her children, the farmer she worked with every day, her business, and now her children were just leaving home. But she knew that she had persevered. She had trusted God; and He had helped her, comforted her, and gave her so much love. She knew that God would continue to lead her on the path He made for her.

The days at Luke were filled with good conversations. He told her how he and Sharon would just pack up the children and go to the Hills for a week. Luke remembered such good times, and he needed to talk about them. Collette told him she was going to be a grandma and he was so happy for her. He also was going to be a grandparent and was very excited at the prospect of it. Both of them were very sad that their spouses were not here to enjoy the grandchildren.

The next Saturday, Aaron and Collette worked on the frame again. They didn't get started on it until late again. Aaron thought it wouldn't take much to get it finished, but he broke the first glass, and then she broke the second glass. Aaron dug up another one somewhere, and they were just going to finish it when company dropped in. Collette ended up visiting with the couple that stopped in, and before they knew it, it was 4:00 a.m. She wanted to just go home and try for another day, but Aaron wanted to finish it. So they did. She came home totally exhausted but glad the project was done. She thought his daughter would really like it, as it turned out very nice, and Aaron had made it.

Collette had a chance to get another maid job. It was for a divorced man who lived only a few miles away. Jake seemed very nice, so she said she would clean for him. Jenni was home on spring break, and it was so good to have her home. They did some shopping together. One night, Jenni picked up two teenage boys who got stuck on a road nearby that was not plowed. Brad went back over there with the loader tractor and got them out. They pooled their money together and came up with $35 to give to Brad. Brad didn't take the money. They were so appreciative and said he had to. Finally, Brad took $5 for gas and told them they should remember this and do something good for someone else. They should also go to church on Sunday.

March 22, 2004

I worked six hours today at one place and then three and a half at another place. When I came home, Brad was finishing chores. We ate supper and went to Howard to get my white car home. Brad had been so worried about money the past week again. When he got into my little white car, the "God" station was on the radio. The first thing he heard was that "God says, don't worry." Brad felt pretty good after that. Just when we got home, Grandma Schock called and said there were some of Dad's cousins there. So Brad and I drove into town to see them. She had just lost her husband and had a twenty-year-old son that lived with her. I tried to be comforting and said there are so many stages of grief. Be good to yourself and give yourself time to deal with all of it. Brad shared how hard it was for him. He said you don't know how hard it is on us kids. I know that Brad goes down to milk at Larry's every so often because he is still grieving the loss of farming with Dad.

March 24, 2004

I started at Jake's house today. His kids came home while I was cleaning. It was the first time I met them. I knew nothing about them, and the son-in-law came in and started visiting with me. I was cleaning a large mirror on the wall of the living room. He asked me where Jake kept his new toy. I said I had no idea, and maybe he took it on the truck with him, not having any idea what he was talking about. Then he found a gun and was looking for bullets. By that time, I was backing up moving toward the mirror and thinking what this was going to look like in slow motion when he shoots me with that pistol, and the blood and glass are flying all over. I think that is when I stepped in the sticky mouse trap. I said he just caught a big one. I had seen these traps all over the house, but I thought they were for crickets. I figured he had a bug problem. When I found out it was a mouse trap, I went a little crazy, and my eyes got huge, much to the amusement of the son-in-law. I said I don't clean houses that have mice in them! I hobbled around with one shoe on and one shoe off until I could get my shoe released from the trap. It was quite the adventure.

By now it was the first of April, and she had not heard from Aaron for a few weeks. She knew that his daughter was getting married that weekend, so she stopped in after work to wish him well at the wedding. He seemed glad to see her. They talked about the wedding for a while and how he missed April going through this wedding. She didn't stay long and then went outside to leave. He followed her. Just then a few geese flew overhead. He said, "You know, geese mate for life."

She said, "I hope the wedding goes well, and they will be very happy. Will you call me when you get back and let me know how it went and if she liked what we made for her?"

He said, "Yes, I'll call you either Sunday night or Monday night."

As she drove away, she knew in her heart that he would not call her like he had said.

Spring work started early in April. Brad started getting the field ready to plant oats. Jenni and Jeff helped get the seed oats. Jenni disked the field. She enjoyed the field work, just like

Collette did. Between Brad and Jenni and Des, they did all the work for oats. Collette came home from work one day and had planned to do the dragging, but it was already done. She told Brad, "I wanted to do a little farming too. I thought I could at least do the dragging for oats, and it was already done when I got home. I lost so much when I lost Dad, and I need to do a little farming."

Brad said, "I lost the chance to farm with Dad, and it's only even if you don't farm."

She told him, "It will never be even. I lost so much more than you did! You still have Des, and you are farming, and you are young with your whole life ahead of you. I have nothing left."

"It was so terribly hard to give up milking!" Brad replied.

"I know it was hard for you. Dad gave it up too. He couldn't milk anymore when he was sick, and it was terribly hard for him too. But this is the way life is now, and we just have accept it the best we can."

That night, she wrote in her journal,

> *I am so empty. I just want to run away and not deal with it anymore. I want to go to California with Char. Maybe we could both start a new life there. Just start over. My heart hurts so very much, and it doesn't seem to get any better. Days just go on, one after another, with new problems to solve, and still no sign of happiness for me. Aaron didn't call tonight like he said he would. I can't even talk to him tonight when I need to talk to someone so desperately. I told God that I am worthless to Him without someone to love me and to make a life with me.*

Collette went back to work at Jake's house. This time, he was home. She was a little nervous as she went inside and started to clean. He started visiting with her, and as soon as she looked into his deep blue eyes, she knew she had nothing to be nervous about. They talked the whole time she cleaned. He was very interesting and interested in what she had to say. He was a farmer too and also did trucking. She thought it was great to talk farming with him.

When Collette got home from work one night, she saw a cow out. She had to set up two blue gates in the lot in order to catch the cow and hold her until Brad got home to take care of it. She tried to move the two gates together, but they were so heavy, and they fell down. She tried to lift them up, but she couldn't budge them. She tried again, and she said, "Merl, help me!" And the gates came up off the ground as if by themselves. She stood them upright. Then she said, "Thanks a lot, Merl! I appreciate that!" And then she looked toward heaven and cried. "I miss you so very much! And I love you, no matter what!" She opened the adjoining gate and got the cow in and did the rest of the chores. Later on, the kids were all home, and they had supper and played cards. She knew that Merl was there with them.

Now it was after Easter and the girls had to go and look for dresses for Brad and Desiree's wedding. They had a great day together. Collette found a beautiful dress for herself for the wedding. It was a size 6, and she could barely get into it. So she ordered the dress in a size 8 for the wedding. She was just thrilled. She knew how proud Merl would be for her to lose the weight like she had done. She could hardly believe she had lost sixty pounds. When she looked into the mirror, she didn't even know who she was. Plans were being made for the wedding, and the date was set for August 21, 2004.

The days of spring brought more work again, and she was outside all the time. She helped with all the chores, and when she didn't, she took walks and enjoyed the beautiful creation God has made. She had not heard from Aaron and wondered what was going on. Why didn't he call her when he had said he would call right after his daughter's wedding? That was three weeks ago now. She decided she was not going to call him. He would have to call her first.

April 25, 2004

I went to church today, and they played "God Will Make a Way." It always makes me cry. I asked Don to be on the committee to pick the next recipient of the Merlin Schock scholarship. He said he would be honored to do it. He is such a good person. I can see it in him. I mentioned to him that I can't get my lawn mower to work. He said he might not know how to fix it, but he has friends who do. He said they would come over soon and take a look at it. Gayle said he will come and mow my whole yard. I told him I can't afford him. He said he never got to do anything for Merl when he was sick, and this is something he can do for me, and he will do it, with absolutely no pay. He is very sweet, and I really appreciate it.

April 29, 2004

I got a nice card today from Aaron's daughter, thanking me for the picture frame that we made. She said she really liked it. But I have

*still heard nothing from Aaron. I am so disap-
pointed in him. I thought we were better friends
than that.*

In May, the day came to give out the Merlin Schock
Scholarship. This time, Mike did an excellent job of delivering
the little speech. Everyone was very happy, and they took pictures again. When she got into the car, Collette expected to hear
"I Believe" on the radio, but she didn't. She searched all over
the stations, looking for the right music, but she didn't find it.
Finally, she cried out, "Please don't leave me, Merl! I still love
you, no matter what."

May was busy with planting and work. Brad was working
and farming and mostly moving ninety miles an hour. He was
working fast and hard, still trying to let go of the deep sense of
grief and loss in his life. He barely made it to the FFA meeting when Mike gave out the scholarship. He planned too many
things in the day, just to keep very busy so he wouldn't think
about Dad, especially on that day.

Collette started working at another house. Blake was a
divorced man also who farmed. He was someone she knew, and
he had a great sense of humor. He usually came in the house for
a little while when she was there, and they always talked farming. She was still having great conversations with Luke also.
Even if he was busy farming, he always took time to come in
and talk to her for a while. He was still in a lot of grief, as it was
still in the first year that his wife had passed away.

Collette went to a high school graduation for Carrie's son.
There were a couple of women there from the grief group, but
not Aaron. She figured he was farming. She was glad she went
to support her friend. Going through these big events without

your spouse, especially for the first time is really hard to do. She knew that it was important to give all the support she could.

At the end of May, Curt's brother passed away from brain cancer. Collette really struggled to go to the funeral. She knew it would remind her so much of what she went through. But she did go to the visitation, and she was glad she did. Curt lost his only brother, just like Larry did. They grew up very poor, just like the Schock family, but at least their family did not have to deal with alcoholism. There were so many similarities, and that's why it made it hard for her to go. Collette knew that Curt's sister-in-law, Bev, would go through a lot of pain.

In May, there was a lot of rain that year. They got crops in, but it was a struggle. By the end of May, she realized that it was two months since she had heard from Aaron. She thought about the last time they saw each other. The geese had flown over, and he said they mate for life. Maybe he was trying to tell her that he could never let go of April. She thought about how he was there for her through the worst time in her life. She knew that God had sent him into her life because she needed him. Maybe now that time was over. She thought about how every time she was so distraught about something, she would run to him. She would say, "This is the most important thing to deal with right now." Then he would always say to her, "No, the most important thing in life is your personal relationship with Christ." And it would bring her back to what is real and what is not. She knew that she would always remember those words.

One day in July, Aaron's parents drove into the yard. They were returning some jars from the pickles and jam she had made for them. They were very polite and kind. She thought maybe they wondered why she had not been around the past few months when, prior to that, she had been with Aaron almost every weekend. But they didn't say a word about it, and she didn't either. A few nights later, she called Aaron. He was so happy to talk to her and was surprised that his parents had been there.

Every day was filled with so much work and stress. Collette had wanted Brad and Des to rent a place in town for a while to give her a little more time on the farm. She didn't know how long she would need to live there, and she was definitely not ready to move out just yet. But Brad didn't want to do that. He wanted to be close to the farm, so they talked to some neighbors and were able to buy an acreage within a mile and a half of her farm. They were busy getting it ready for them to live in after the wedding in August.

The third of August, high winds and a hailstorm came through. Mike called very upset that his oats crop was gone, and a silage wagon was tipped over. At Collette's farm, there was damage too. Trees were down, the windbreak broke, and the corn looked sick. Later that day, Aaron came. He had planned to come and fix the doors on the house that night. But, first, he helped clean up some mess and assessed the damage. It was dark by the time they started on the project they had planned to work on. He had supper with the family. Collette invited him to come to the reception for Brad's wedding. He said he would like to come.

The days of August flew by. She was working in the Tieszen house one day when she heard the Tim McGraw song "Live Like You Were Dying" on her little radio. Collette saw pictures in her mind. She saw Merl sitting in the chair when the optometrist said he had melanoma and would lose his eye. She saw the doctor that said interferon wasn't working, then at the Mayo clinic when they said there's nothing they can do. Then she saw Merl desperately trying to get things ready before he died. He bought machinery and talked to the lawyer and the banker. And then how he was such a sweet patient, appreciative of everything anyone did for him. He never complained, and he accepted his fate with grace and dignity. She missed him so very much. She thought how there can never be anyone else who can take his place and she would be lonely the rest of her life.

August 18, 2004

I woke up and thought about it being our anniversary today. I just want him back, but I know I can't have him. I have to learn to go on with life. In the evening, Aaron was supposed to come and help finish up the doors that still don't work. I needed new locks. He called and said he can't come, he just has too much work to do. I told him I was going to give him the invitation to Brad's wedding but ended up explaining directions to him on the phone instead. I told him he didn't have to come to the wedding if he didn't want to. But he said he would. When I hung up the phone, at first I didn't know what to do. I had to be able to lock the doors when I left for Brad's wedding in a couple of days. I remembered that Don had said he would do anything for me, all I had to do was ask. So I called him. He said he wasn't doing much, and he came right over. He had his brother with him. They devoured the supper I had made for Aaron and then worked on my locks. They needed more tools than they had, so said they would come back tomorrow.

The next morning, promptly at 7:30 a.m., the two brothers were back with the right tools. They enjoyed the coffee and bars Collette had and finished the job in a short time. She was so relieved she could lock the doors when she was gone a couple of days. Then she went to Mike's place and helped them cut hay silage. Mike was so relieved to get done that night.

August 21, 2004

Brad and Desiree's wedding—Brad got up early to milk at Larry's. I got up and talked with him a little before he left. Jenni was not home, as she had stayed at Des's house overnight. Brad left at 5:30 a.m. Suddenly the house became very quiet. I drank some coffee, and then it hit me. My heart ached so much I couldn't stand it. I cried for about an hour. We raised those kids together, diapers, late nights, and went through all the worries. Now he should be here for the good part too. My heart was just broken into a million pieces again. When I finally got myself together, I finished packing and showered and left for Mitchell. I called Carrie. She was so good to talk to about it all, and she made me feel better. I knew I had to get through the day and a long evening too. At the wedding, the ceremony was so funny and touching and Des fought back the tears. Brad was comical and so charming and full of love. It was wonderful.

It was so cool to see the bride and groom drive his combine from the church to the reception in Lennox. Brad was so proud of his new bride. The church and reception were crowded, and it was difficult to get to talk to people. My college friends were there, and they were a great support. They told me I looked beautiful and really boosted my spirits. At the dance, Aaron suddenly showed up beside me. I was surprised. He said he had been so sick. He spent Thursday and Friday in bed and was just feeling better today. I asked him why he didn't say he was sick on Wednesday when we talked, but he said he didn't know he was sick then. I introduced him to my college friends. and he visited with them awhile. When they left at 11:30, he wanted to leave too. I asked him to dance with me, but he wouldn't. Then Aaron left. A short time later, Larry told me that he can't get his car started, and my nephew Travis was going to jump it. I went out to see what was going on. Travis was trying to jump it, but it just didn't seem to work. Finally, Jeff came over and locked and unlocked the doors, and then it started right up. Then the rest left, and Aaron and I were left alone. He finally remembered the door locks and asked if I got them fixed. I told him that I called Don, and he came right over and didn't get it done that night. I had told Don that I know he doesn't have time to come back the next day yet to finish it, but Don said he would make time.

I was so glad to have it done before this wedding, so I could lock the house. After Aaron left, I went back inside. I felt so alone with no one to dance with. Merl was such a good dancer. He would have loved to visit and dance and be at this wedding. But I know in my heart that he was there somewhere, somehow.

The days that followed the wedding were exhausting. Collette went back to work. Brad and Des came back from a honeymoon on August 26. They worked on moving more of Brad's things into their house, and that night would be their first night in their new home together. The evening of August 26, Mike and Joann had their baby boy. They called him Jonathon Michael. He was small, as he had come two weeks early. The family all went to see Jonathon that night. It made Collette sad to have this new grandbaby without Merl there to experience it too. But she was sure that Merl had held this baby before he came to earth.

August 27, 2004

Jeff and I helped Jenni move back to Brookings for college today. While we were there, Mike called and said that Jonathon was moved to Sioux Falls Hospital because his lungs were not developed enough, and they don't have the equipment in Mitchell to handle it. Jenni and I took her car to Sioux Falls to meet Mike with the ambulance. Jeff took the pickup home and brought my red car to Sioux Falls. When we got to the hospital in Sioux Falls, Mike looked so worried. He had rode along with the ambulance from Mitchell to Sioux Falls. The baby was in an incubator and was hooked up to all these tubes. He looked awful. My heart just ached to look at him. My heart hurt for Mike too. I told him I can't do anything to help Jonathon, but I can sit here with him, keep him company and pray. They came out and told us that he will be all right. He just needs time. We stayed overnight a few hours at Pat and Curt's house.

August 30, 2004

It's two years today that Merl is gone. I still don't understand it. How can he not be here? We have a new grandbaby. He's in the hospital, and our family needs Merl more than ever. I am so alone to do all of these things, first the wedding and now the grandchild. I worked all day, but it was hard to keep my mind on what I was doing. Then I wanted to see Jonathon so much, so I called Mike. He said I should go. When I got there, Joann was sleeping in her room, so I went to see the baby. I held his hand and rubbed his feet and talked to him until he fell asleep. I was there almost an hour. Then I went to find Joann and gave her some money for meals, and I went home. Later, Brad and Des and I put up fence in the oats field. It was a beautiful night with a full moon. I felt Merl there with us, somehow. I miss him so very much and I still love him.

September 2, 2004

I worked at the Tieszen house all day. After work, I raced home and went over to Brad's place. He showed me the house. It looks really nice, and I think it will be a good place for them. Brad and I went to Sioux Falls to see Jonathon. He was moved to a different floor and is starting to nurse now. Jenni and Jeff came up today too. Des also stopped. On the way home, I was still so sad. I tried to figure out why I am so sad with this baby. Is it because Merl is not here to be Grandpa? Is it because it means that life moves on even though he is not here? Or am I sad because there is so much change in my life and I don't have any control over it? I guess I really don't know. I do know that I love that little baby, and he will always be a very import-ant part of my life. I tried to call Carrie, but she didn't answer tonight.

The next day, Collette went back to Luke. She had not been there in a month, as he had been traveling. She thought it was so good to see him again. The first thing he asked was, "How was the wedding?"

"It was good, but I cried for an hour in the morning. I just couldn't help it. I missed Merl so very much," she said.

She told him about the new grandson and how he was in the hospital. She told him she was so sad about the baby and no Merl. He told her that Sharon would have loved to be there for this first grandchild. Collette knew that the next day would be the first anniversary of Sharon's death. He said he was going to leave for the Hills tomorrow with some friends over the weekend. She thought that was a good plan. Then he went into the living room and fell asleep on the chair. He was still so exhausted from being gone for four weeks. She knew that he was just trying to get away from all the pain he was experiencing. The memories are at home, and being somewhere else is a good place to be on these tough days. He said he needs to buy a new combine, but he really doesn't care. He will just hire it done this year. The two of them had always farmed together, just like Merl and Collette. She knew what kind of pain he was experiencing.

Saturday night, Jenni and Collette went to a Gretchen Wilson and Martina McBride concert at the fairgrounds in Huron. The weather looked very threatening, and after Martina started singing, it started to rain. She kept singing, even when it started to rain quite heavily. Collette and Jenni wrapped up in a blanket and then remembered they had an umbrella. So they used the umbrella too. Most of the people around them had left by this time, but they thought if she was still singing, they didn't want to miss it. When it was over, they made a run for the buildings and waited until it let up. By the time they got to the car, they were soaking wet. They went through the drive up at McDonald's and waited for a half-hour to get something to eat. By this time, Jenni was quite frazzled. They headed home, and about twenty minutes later, she got stopped by the cop for speeding. He gave her a warning ticket. After he left, she told Collette it was her third one and opened the glove compartment to shove it in there. Collette was not happy and said, "Mental note to self. Make sure I drive next time!"

They had a great time together. It was so good for both of them.

When Collette went back to Luke, she knew that he had a rough time getting through the first anniversary of Sharon's death. His friends were good for him, but he was just so sad. She knew exactly how he felt. She wished she could be more help to him in his grief.

September 13, 2004

My birthday. I worked today and then twisted my hip and was in such pain I had to quit an hour later. I went home, took some ibuprofen, and slept for a couple of hours. I felt somewhat better and went out to see how the guys were doing with the silage cutting. Brad went to work at the vet in the afternoon, and then I took his place hauling silage. We got twenty-nine loads on the pile today. Des came after work, and Jenni brought me an angel food cake and strawberries. Mike grilled hamburgers, and we had supper here. They gave me a griddle, so I guess they still expect me to cook. It was great to see Jonathon again too. In the eve in the eastern sky, I saw a beautiful rainbow. I knew immediately it was from Merl, wishing me a happy birthday. He used to bring me red roses. Now he sends me rainbows. I cried. I still miss him so very much. Maybe he is telling me to be happy in this life. I just need someone to love me again—to love me like he did. I had a pretty good birthday. My kids still love me. I was hauling silage with the 560, and Merl sent me a rainbow. How can it get any better than that!

Late in September, they started combining beans. There was weather to fight and lots of late nights again. It rained when they did not have beans done, so they went to do some corn and finished beans later. Also had breakdowns along the way. Collette still had lots of maid work to do, and so all the late nights with farming were hard to keep up with. But she loved the farming part with her children. And whenever she was home alone and not farming, she would clean house. It was therapy for her.

While Collette and the boys were out in the field combining one night, they heard of the loss of a young woman in the community. She had died in a car accident. They all knew her and were so sad at such a tremendous loss. After harvest was over, Collette went to see the parents. She wrote in her journal,

November 8, 2004

I cleaned today and then came home and finished mowing lawn. Then I did chores. Brad came at 4:00 p.m. and we went out to combine. I took the corn test to Canova and was so happy when they told me it was 14.9. I don't think they have ever seen a woman so happy about a moisture test! I came home and was moving wagons for Brad when he got stuck with the combine. We were both a wreck. I prayed that God would help us, and He did. We pulled it out from the front, and I was so thankful. It was almost dark by then. Brad went home and I came in the house. I called the family that lost their daughter and asked if I could bring a pan of bars. My stomach hurt, and I was so ner-

vous. I prayed all the way over there that God would tell me what to say or do. The whole family was there when I came. I told them how a grief group had helped me. I gave them a list of places that have grief support groups. I told them about being angry and crying out to God on top of my pickup. Mostly I told them about my own experiences of loss. The father said that Don was there and had talked about the loss of his daughter. Before I left, I played the tape of "I Can Only Imagine" by Mercy Me. When it was over, I said their daughter doesn't have to imagine anymore, she is with God. And the best part is that we will see her again. When the dad walked me to my car, he said I didn't need to leave just yet, so I felt that maybe it was okay that I was there. I was so scared to do it, but I felt good about it.

At Luke's farm the next day, Collette helped him move his auger and tractor down the road. She often helped him move equipment from one field to another. He had bought a new combine and was combining his own crops. She told him about her experience with the family who lost a daughter. Luke had told her of a group in Mitchell that meets because of the loss of a child. She had given them that information.

The middle of November, Mike and Brad were still combining corn. They had breakdowns, and so when they could go, they did, until two in the morning. The corn was broke over from the wind they had earlier, and so they had to combine one way in the field. Collette helped as much as she could. They all got so tired.

> November 19, 2004
>
> *I cleaned today and came home early to help combine. I climbed into the skidloader to do the chores, and I saw something moving by my feet. When I looked down, I saw the mouse. I'm sure the people in Spencer heard my scream. I made some sandwiches later and headed over to Mike's. We started combining by 6:30 and had three loads by 9:30 when it started to rain. I just wanted to cry. We barely get going, and we either have a breakdown or it rains. Mike is taking it pretty good. I don't know how he takes all this stress. I came home at 11:00 p.m.*

On Thanksgiving, the family got together with Collette's family. They took four-generation pictures with Mike and Jonathon. Collette thought how they could never take them with Merl's side of the family now since Merl was gone. In December, she had a Christmas gathering for the Schock family. It felt good to be together, but it was so hard on Merl's parents. There is just such a big hole in the family now. Merl was always so much fun at these gatherings.

The grief group got together in December. Aaron was there, and he made a special effort to visit with Collette. He asked about harvest and her children. He told her she should call him. But Collette knew that the phone works both ways, and he had not called her since Brad's wedding in August.

Right after Christmas, Jenni had wisdom teeth removed. She had an awful time with it, as she had a stress attack when she came out of anesthesia. Later on, she got dry socket, and Collette ended up taking her to Sioux Falls on New Year's Eve. At 2:00 a.m., they arrived in Sioux Falls, and the doctor came in to give her medicine. It was 4:00 a.m. by the time they got home and crawled into bed. Jenni and Collette were both so depressed by then. They were just glad to have another year over.

Aunt Jenni holding Jon and Marah

Chapter 7

2005 – More Change

January 1, 2005

We slept from 4:00 a.m. to 10:30 a.m. We ate a little bit and then went back to bed. We both slept until 3:00 p.m. Jenni and I were both so depressed all day. It was sleeting here by 11:00 a.m. I called Pat, and she said it had been ice there from early a.m., and their cars were coated. I was so glad I took Jenni in the middle of the night, as I don't know how I could have driven the roads on the sheet of ice. I was so glad to have her feel better too. I was still mad that the doctors didn't want to come in any earlier on NYE. She should have had relief sooner than what she did! Jeff came out in the evening tonight, and she was so glad to see him. Another year is starting, and no happiness in sight for me. I have prayed and prayed that God will give me someone to love, someone to love me. I played "I Can Only Imagine" tonight. I just had to cry.

I want to go to heaven. There isn't anything here for me. I can't bear all this unhappiness. Where is that e-mail, God?

January 3, 2005

I didn't want to get out of bed this morning. It was so cold. But I did anyway and then went and cleaned a house. I called Gary Wieman today to come out and put a price on my machinery. He said he would be glad to come and do that for us. Brad wants to buy my machinery. After I got off the phone, I just burst into tears. It is one more thing I have to let go of. I can't stand this anymore. I just can't! No one seems to understand what this means to me. No one would, except Merl. Sometimes, it seems so long ago already, and I should be able to move on. But I just can't. I guess I don't want to. I cried a long time this afternoon, trying to free myself of this terrible pain in my heart. But it just doesn't go away. It's not fair that I have to lose everything. It was bad enough to lose Merl. Brad took Jenni to the doctor to repack her dry socket today. This evening, we went to get Jenni's car, and it is not fixed. They put in a torque converter, and it didn't fix it. Now she is worried it is the transmission. It never ends. In the eve, I worked on papers and cleaning out files. It is boring, but it has to be done. I am so tired of just doing what I have to. I am young enough to

*want to have some fun in life, and there never is
any. There is never any happiness.*

A couple of days later, it snowed. The roads were covered
with snowpack, but they had to go back to Sioux Falls
again to have the dry socket repacked. It hurt Jenni so
bad she had tears roll down her cheeks. By this time, Collette
was very upset that Jenni should have to be so miserable for so
long. That ended up being the last time she had to have the dry
socket packed. And she finally got better. Jenni went back one
more time but just had the packets removed and used ibuprofen
after that.

The next weekend, Collette was tired of being alone all
weekend, so she called her friend Carrie from the grief group.
Carrie said they could meet in Mt. Vernon for supper. The
two women had lots to catch up on, and they visited all night.
Carrie said she would like to have someone in her life again
too. Collette told how she had been so depressed, and life just
seems to keep going on with nothing to look forward to. Jenni
had gone into town to see Jeff, and when she came home, she
couldn't find the key to the house. Jenni called Collette but
still could not find it. So Collette headed for home. Carrie told
Collette she should leave home more often.

Sunday, Jenni had to go back to college. She really didn't
want to go. She knew she would miss her mom, and Mom
would miss her too. They had a lot of bonding time while she
was in pain over the vacation. Brad came over after she left.
Collette told him that she was still so sad. Brad told her that
they didn't want to hear about Dad anymore, because it was
such a downer, and then they think they must feel sorry for her.
Collette wrote in her journal,

January 9, 2005

I can't help it that I am sad. Losing Merl totally changed my life. Sometimes, I don't even know who I am without him. I feel like I am just in the kids' way, and they wish I would have died with Dad. I guess a part of me did. But I can't take it if my children are against me. That's all I have left down here. I still want to go home to heaven. It would be the best for everyone. No, I know it would only be the best for me. My children need me whether they know it or not. And they will need me for a long time.

The next day, she went to Luke and helped him take down his Christmas tree. They had a good time together. He was fun to be around. Just before she left, his daughter came. She told Collette that she looked different. Collette told her that she had lost sixty pounds and let her hair grow out of the perm. From there, she went to another house to clean and drove into Mitchell for groceries. She decided to wash the car, as it was quite warm for January. After she washed it, she wiped down the doors with towels that she kept in the car. When she got home, she decided she had better wipe them off some more so they don't freeze shut. So she tried to open the back door. It wouldn't come open. Then she tried the other back door. Same thing, wouldn't budge. Then in a panic, she was beating on the front door when she realized the doors were locked. It felt good to laugh at herself.

On the weekend, Jenni came home. It was so good to have her back home again. They had a good time together, and Jenni helped her do some cleaning. Later on Saturday afternoon,

Collette and Brad went to the Madison sale barn to try to bid on some stock cows. It was standing room only there, and they didn't even get to bid. The next week, they went to Mitchell sale barn but didn't get any stock cows there either. They were just too expensive.

February 4, 2005

Friday. It was a beautiful day today for Merl's fifty-third birthday. I had a candle burning for him in the morning. Then I went to clean at Luke. He was just leaving for two days. He seemed so sad today. Another year has gone by since he lost Sharon. I feel so bad for him. I have been there. While I was cleaning in his house, I heard on the radio "Amazed by You" by Lonestar. Merl used to sing that song in the barn. I always felt he was singing it to me. On the way home today, I heard "There's No Way" by Alabama. They never play that song on the radio anymore. It is from the 1980s. I knew it was from Merl, and I just cried. I miss him, and I still love him so very much. I will always love him. Jenni brought me a rose today. That was so sweet of her. I need her so much these days. We really bonded over Christmas vacation when she was so miserable with her teeth. Tonight Don called me for Brad's phone number. He was so upset about losing his daughter and going through the divorce. He said nothing good can ever come out of it. I told him it is your choice what you do with your life after something bad happens. I told him about Abraham who wanted children and was so old when he finally got Isaac. Then he was supposed to sacrifice him. Because he was willing to do what God said, he was blessed many times over. Look at the trials of Job. He lost everything, but he still had faith in God. It is all a test of faith that we go through here on earth. Are we going to choose God no matter what? If we do, He will bless us and take us home to be with Him eternally. And that is really the only thing that matters. We had a good conversation about it all.

The next day, Don met Brad in Salem, and they worked on getting planter parts. That week, they worked on the planter almost every day. Don had made a ten-row planter out of an eight-row. He had also made a ten-row corn head for his combine. Now he was helping Brad change his planter into a ten-row. Brad was so glad to have someone to work with who knew how to fix things. He enjoyed his time with Don. Collette sent some food along with Brad for him and Don those days, as she was so thankful that Don took the time to help them.

Brad and Des went to Madison and bought some cows. They were solid mouth cows, and they got a good deal on them. Collette bought some too. They were still trying to build up the stock cow herd. Collette found some buyers and pieced out the milking equipment. She knew it would never be used on that farm again and felt she should get a few dollars out of it before it deteriorated completely. It was hard to see the empty milk house, especially for Brad.

Carrie called one afternoon. They had a good long conversation. She said that Aaron had called her. He was doing okay. After she got off the phone, Collette thought about Aaron. She had not thought about him for some time now. He was always so interesting, and they had such deep conversations. She knew she had not called him because she was handling things better and getting stronger. Sometimes, people are in your life for a season for a special purpose. She knew that Aaron had been in her life for a very special reason.

By the beginning of April, the little calves were running around the pasture with their tails high in the air. Collette loved to watch them. The warm weather made everyone feel better. And work on the farm started to move forward. They got machinery ready and soon were ready to plant oats. Collette helped with some field work.

Late in April, Don asked Collette to help him order a stone for his daughter's grave. In 2000, Don's little girl died from a poisonous gas that worked its way from crushed rock around the house into the sump pump. She was just a few days shy of six years old when she died. Her name was Bridget, and she was a very precious little girl. She would sing her heart out with her two older sisters when they did special music in church. She knew that God loved her, and you could see it in her. After the little girl died, Don's wife took their two other daughters and moved out, and since then, they had been divorced. Don had been through a very rough time. He not only lost his daughter. He also lost his two other children and his marriage. He survived all of it because of his love for God and his knowledge that Jesus died for his sins. He knew that Bridget was in heaven and he would see her again someday. There was so much pain in the years since then, but now he was ready to place a stone on her grave, and he knew Collette would be good to help him with that. They met at Mitchell that day and went to several different places until he found the one he knew was right. That same day, he also picked out two new twin beds for his daughters, Rachel and Renae, for when they would stay at his house. He had not seen them for some time and missed them very much.

Don also asked Collette to clean house for him. She spent many days cleaning, and then some friends came to help paint the house so that it would look nice when Don's daughters came to see him. He was so nice to her, and she felt he was coming on too strong, so one of the days she was cleaning, she told him that she needed a man with a boat, thinking that would take care of it. She didn't think there was any way he had a boat. But to her surprise, Don said, "I have a boat!"

Collette's face fell immediately. She slowly said, "You do?"

"Yes, I have a boat!" he said, rather proudly.

"Where is it?" she said.

"I'll show it to you," Don said excitedly.

He took her to the garage and opened the door, and there it was... a 12 foot jon boat on a small trailer.

She said, "That's not a boat!"

Don stated, "Technically, it is a boat! I won this boat, and I've never used it."

"I had a different kind of boat in mind, one you can actually use," she said.

"We can use this boat on the Big Lake," he said.

"I think I'll pass on that right now," she said.

Collette was still working very long days cleaning houses. She would come home and help the boys with the farming too. She had decided to sell the IHC 706 gas tractor. It had been a loader tractor on the farm for many years. Collette cleaned it up and got it ready for the Wieman sale in Marion. She remembered how Merl and Brad had left the yard with that tractor in a blinding snowstorm to go and look for Merl's parents who were stranded on the road. She remembered picking up bales in the alfalfa field, bedding cows, and feeding cows.

Collette wrote in her journal,

May 24, 2005

I cleaned two houses today and called Brad on the way home. He said Mike is done planting beans and he is coming over here with the disk to do Brad's forty acres yet. So I went home and waited for Mike. He came over about 4:30, and I gave him some lunch. Then I went over to Brad and fed his bottle calves. I disked from 6:00 p.m. until I got it done, about 8:00 p.m. I heard "I Believe" by Diamond Rio in the tractor, and I cried. I still miss Merl so much. Tomorrow, I will have to sell the 706. Merl never liked that tractor and would have been happy to see it go. But for some reason, it hurts me to do it. I guess it is just another little piece of Merl that is gone. I am trying so hard to move on, but it is hard to let go. By 8:00 p.m. Mike had the planter here, and Brad was home too. Brad tried to plant, but he couldn't see the marker. Bad weather was all around us tonight, and it got dark early. The planter marker didn't work, and the boys were trying to figure out how to fix it. I sat in Brad's pickup, and I remembered the boys at four and five, at eight and

*nine, and at thirteen and fourteen. As the tears
rolled down my cheeks, I prayed that God would
let them figure out what they needed to do to fix
it. They needed each other all those years, and
they still need each other so much now. In just
a few minutes, they had it figured out and were
moving again. Brad took me over to Mike's to
get my car home and then took more beans out
to Mike. I finally went to bed about 11:00 p.m.
It was another emotional day.*

At the sale, she was surprised that the 706 sold as well as
it did. It went to a farmer from Nebraska who wanted to use
it to rake hay. It was another little piece of Merl and Collette's
lives together, gone. Moving on. And she knew that she should
be too.

In May, the Schock family gave out another Merlin Schock
scholarship. It always felt good to help someone with their college expenses. The whole family usually came to the FFA banquet to give out the award.

When Memorial Day came, Collette went up to the church
to put flowers on Merl's grave. She stopped to see Bridget's
grave. She told Bridget, "Your dad has bought a stone for you,
and it will be very nice. He is getting his life together now, and
he will be all right."

Then she walked over to Merl's grave and placed the red
roses nearby. Collette loved red roses, and she always wanted
Merl to bring her some. He did as often as he could. Now she
was taking them to him. She told him, "I still miss you, and I
love you no matter what. I always will. I just don't understand
what the plan is. Have I made a difference for anyone down

here, God? I just don't know that I have. Yet I'm sure you have a plan. I just pray you will have another man who will love me the rest of my days. I am so lonely."

The next week, she went to see Luke again. They talked about Memorial Day. Luke said his children were home to help him get through the day. She helped him move equipment to different fields. They had a good time together, and he appreciated her help.

June 1, 2005

In the early a.m., I looked out my kitchen window and saw a skunk. It looked rabid because it was wobbling across the yard. I called Jenni, and we tried to get the rifle to take bullets. I sneaked outside and tried to pull the trigger, but it wouldn't go. So I ran back into the house and called Roger, and he came with the shotgun. He said it isn't often that you drive by a farm with a woman outside with a gun in her hands. He shot the skunk, and it rolled under a pile of trees. He must have been a grandpa because he was huge, almost as big as a badger. And I bet he was helping himself to cat food. I told Roger I owe him a pan of bars. Then I left to clean a house, but the second job canceled. She said they have not been home much. I thought that was strange as I didn't know what difference it made. I know their house is a mess the minute I leave, with their two energetic little boys. About 12:30, the phone rang, and it was Ann. Then I knew why I had a cancelation.

Ann was finally ready to talk. She had received the card from me on the one year anniversary of her husband's death. She said she can't take the thought of twenty years of being alone. I said not to think of it that way. Just try to get through the week or even the day. Plan things to look forward to. We had just had a day of trimming trees and yard work. Pat and Curt had come, and we spent the whole day working. It was good therapy, and I had looked forward to it. I tried to be comforting and encouraging to her. I could tell she really needed it, so I was glad I was home to answer the phone. In the evening, Don called just to talk. He is getting his girls for short periods of time and was so happy to see them. He even wanted to take me out for supper. I said yes, so we will go to Pizza Ranch with the neighbors on Sunday night.

Sunday night came. Collette was looking forward to her "date" with Don. He showed up at the door, and Jenni was there with Collette. He visited with Jenni for a while, and then Brad stopped in. Then he talked farming with Brad. Collette was thinking that he was trying to get her kids to see his good side before he would win her over. He must be a pretty smart guy. They finally left and went to the neighbors. They had a lot of fun with Tom and Mary that night. Two weeks later, Don asked Collette to go along to a wedding he was invited to. She went with him, and they had a great time with lots of mutual friends at the wedding. Still, she just didn't know that it was smart to get involved with this guy. He was divorced and had so much going on in his life. Would he really have time or energy for her? Could he love her the way Merl did?

The end of June Collette was home alone, and Jeff drove in the yard. She met him at the door and said, "Jeff, what are you doing here? Jenni is at work today."

"I know. I came to see you," he said.

"Oh, oh... Come on in," Collette replied.

He came into the living room, and they sat down to talk.

Jeff said, "I think it is time."

He showed Collette the engagement ring he had with him. It was beautiful.

"That's huge for Jenni's little fingers!"

"But it's absolutely beautiful, and she will love it!" Collette exclaimed.

They talked for almost two hours. Jeff said he was going to buy his grandpa's house in Salem. He said he would promise to take care of her always. Collette gave Jeff her blessing and told him he is already part of the family. After he left, Collette started thinking of Jenni's wedding plans and what it would be like to live here without her. She would miss her so very much. They had been through so much together, but now Jenni would start a new adventure in life with Jeff. Collette knew that Jeff loved Jenni, and it would be good. Later that night, Don called. He had spent a couple of hours with his girls, and he was so happy. They had such a great time together and were so happy to see him. She told him about Jeff's visit. They both knew that things were changing, and changing for the better. Jenni came home about 11:30 that night and woke Collette to show her the ring. Jeff had taken her over to the house he was going to buy from Grandpa to give her the ring. She was so happy!

The next weeks and months were filled with wedding plans for Jenni and Jeff. It was stressful but also lots of fun. Their wedding date was set for July 8, 2006. Mike got married in 2002, Brad in 2004 and now Jenni in 2006. At least the weddings were two years apart. Mike's little Jonathon was born in August of 2004, and he was the joy of Collette's life. Mike and Joann were expecting another child, a girl, due in October of 2005. The family was growing, but it still had a huge hole in the middle of it.

July 4, Collette's family came to the farm. They all had a great time together. Collette invited Don, and he came too. It was the first time Don met Collette's family. Collette's brother, Randy, and Don got the go-cart going again when it broke down. They were the heroes of the day! They all ate too much sheep chislic and enjoyed some fireworks in the evening. Everyone enjoyed the day.

The next weekend, Collette went to see her cousin Nina in Minnesota. They stayed at a bed and breakfast and went shopping in the Cities. It was so good to have the time together just to talk. Collette needed a break from everything going on at home, and a visit with her cousin was just what she needed.

Collette and Jenni started cleaning Jeff's house. It was quite overwhelming as it needed a lot of work to make it a home for Jeff and Jenni. When Collette got home, Brad told her that the bull was gone. They had paid a lot for a black angus bull, but he was so wild; he jumped all the fences and was gone. Collette was so upset that their money just got up and ran away.

The next day, Collette came home from cleaning jobs, and Mike was there. So they went up to the seventeen-acre pasture where the bull was seen last. It had a large slough in the middle of it and a creek that was shallow enough to cross at a certain point. It also held a stock dam. Brad took one pickup, and Mike drove another one, and Collette rode along with Mike. (She felt safer with Mike driving than Brad!) They drove around in all the tall weeds by the stock dam. They figured it was so hot, and he had to be there somewhere. Pretty soon, he popped up. He looked like a wild animal. He had the bowed back of an old horse, and his head was as high as it could go. The whites of his eyes could be seen from a long ways away, and he took off like a bullet. Mike drove as fast as he could and headed him off from the neighbor's fence. The bull found a gate and went into the next pasture closer to home. Brad and Mike used the pickups to guide him south toward home. Once he headed back north and Mike went after him. Brad hollered, "Don't hit him!" At first Collette thought he didn't want Mike to hit him with that pickup. But Brad just wanted to do it himself! The bull would run like a deer and then suddenly stop. He would look at them as if to say, "No, I don't want to go there, and you can't make me!" They waited. Finally, they got him within a few feet of the gate and waited again. Suddenly, he took off toward the west field and blew right through the barbed wire fence. He turned south there and went straight through the oats field. Brad had followed him with the 1986 Chevy pickup down the creek and back up again, and he drove through the hole the bull made in the fence. Now Brad was in hot pursuit going through the oats field that was as tall as the window on the side. The bull came out the south gate and flew right across the road into the corn in the next field. They knew they were done now. They would have to wait for the bull to come out of the cornfield. Brad went home to try to blow chaff out of the pickup radiator. Collette said, "The only thing we can do now is shoot him. His name is Bullet, and he's going to get one!" But then Mike spotted him. He came out of the cornfield and went east headed for Grandpa's quarter. Mike put the pedal down and went past him while he was still in the west ditch. By the time they turned around, he was in the ditch on the east side of the road, going north toward home. The heck with blowing off chaff. Brad saw the action and was back. He drove into the beans in Grandpa's quarter alongside the bull. They were taking him home now. But he had other plans. Suddenly, he turned around and crossed the road and flew back into the cornfield. This time, it was all over. He didn't come out again, at least not until the next day. He was spotted later the next day in with the Schock cattle on Grandpa's quarter. The fence worked perfectly. He must have cleared it somewhere. After it was all over, Brad drove down the road with the 1986 pickup, and they heard a loud bang, like a shotgun. It was the pickup. They towed it to town to fix the next day.

After all that excitement, it was back to work as usual. After work, Jenni and Collette went to clean at Jeff's house again. They both worked until late and then came home and fell into bed.

Collete went to Luke to clean. He thought it was pretty funny to hear about their "wild bull" story. He took Collette to lunch in Mitchell just so he could hear all about it.

Brad and Mike were starting to harvest oats. The first day, they broke down with the combine. The boys were so discouraged. Early the next day, the mechanic from town came out and fixed it as it was a relatively easy fix. They were relieved that they could combine again.

Collette wrote in her journal,

July 23, 2005

I tried to get something done in the house today, but the minute I started something, Brad would call and need me to bring out the 1086 and move the wagon, etc. It was terribly hot today, 105 heat index. I'm amazed the combine worked at all. In the evening, I took back the chairs I had borrowed from the church. I went over to Merl's grave, and I sat there for at least a half an hour. I told him that everything has gone downhill since he left. It is such a struggle every day. But he would love his grandson and the granddaughter that is coming. It was peaceful to sit there today. The wind was blowing, and for once the mosquitoes didn't eat me up. I'm still so confused. Luke is so nice to me, and he's lots of fun. Jake is so interesting to visit with, and Don looks at me in such a special way. Still I just don't know. I just want you, Merl!

The last weekend in July, Collette and her college friends went to Omaha. Jo, Deanna, Linda, Rhonda, LaVetta, and Collette had been together since they were in college at Dakota State in the early 1970s. They had been through everyone's marriages, divorce, babies, children weddings, grandchildren—all of it—together. Now Collette was the first one of the group to lose her husband to cancer. They wanted to have some time with Collette and keep her going in such a hard time in her life. She had time to talk with each one individually, and it was a precious time to her. They went shopping and ate in nice restaurants and had lots of fun together. All too soon, the weekend was over, and they came back home. Brad called Collette on the way home. He said he had a terrible time to load the wild bull, but he got him unloaded at Yankton. The man who unloaded him knew right away he was wild and got out of the way when he came through. At least, now he would not be a problem anymore.

August days were busy. Collette helped Don put up sweet corn. They walked his fields together, and she was impressed at how he was a good farmer and knew so much about farming. They went to a movie in Sioux Falls. He went to a movie with his friend Jerry, and Collette went to a different movie with Jerry's wife, Barb. Afterward, they went out to eat and all had a great time.

Later in August, Brad told Collette that he was going to work full-time in Sioux Falls. He said he needed the money, and he knew it would be a good job for him. Collette was devastated. How would they function without Brad out on the farm every day? Silage cutting was coming soon, and then there would be harvest. How could they get it all done?

September 2, 2005

Luke gave me a raise today. That's so sweet of him. He doesn't know that I actually raised my rates a while ago but didn't have the heart to tell him. He must have known that I needed more money. Don took me to a Def Leppard concert last night. It was wonderful, even though I don't care much for that kind of music. Still it was great to be there with him. He made it so much fun. But on the way home, his legs cramped up, and he could hardly drive. Guess he is still an old man after all.

The next weekend was Labor Day, and the Schocks cut silage. They had plenty of help on the weekend, but then there was still silage to cut, and everyone had to go back to work, including Brad. Collette prayed at work that Mike would be able to get some silage cut even though he was alone to do it. When she got done for the day, she called him. He was in good spirits, as he had got some neighbors and friends to help him. They got a lot done that day. Collette recognized another answer to prayer. Silage cutting continued, and they worked at it until it got done again for another year. Collette drove the 560 tractor when she could. But it made her sad, and she remembered good times with Merl.

She wrote in her diary,

September 17, 2005

I let Jenni drive the 560 today, as I know it is stress relief for her. This afternoon, I was just overcome with grief for Merl again. What is wrong with me? It is three years already, and the sting of pain is just as strong as if it was yesterday. I am just so tired of all the pain. I guess silage and driving the 560 remind me of such good times together. We never did have very much, but we had each other, and that was all that counted. Now that is all gone. There is so much other stuff going on too. Our baby is getting married. Jenni wanted her dad to walk her down the aisle. She can't have that now. She doesn't say too much about it, but I can see it is on her mind. I will have to go through another wedding without him. It is just not right. How can any of this be right? I called Carrie tonight. I told her I feel like I am regressing instead of moving on with life. She said she went through that too. She thinks a part of us is afraid that we will go on with life and forget them. But I don't believe that can ever happen. I want to be happy again. Does that mean I have to forget Merl to do it? I don't believe that. She says she does not want to be alone for the rest of her life either. I have felt that way from the beginning. I got back on the treadmill tonight. It felt good! Then I listened to some of my sad tapes and decided it was time to put them away.

September 29, 2005

Don called me tonight. He is leaving tomorrow to go elk hunting in the Black Hills. He will be gone at least five to six days. I told him people die and are buried in five days, and he should call me sometime while he is gone. He said phone service is bad in the Hills, and he didn't promise he would call.

On September 30, Collette went to clean two houses like always. At noon, Brad called and said that Grandma and Grandpa Schock were in the hospital because of some kind of poisoning. Collette left work and went to Sioux Falls. She found Larry and Judy in the waiting room of intensive care. They did not get to see Irene until about 4:00 p.m. She was so bloated and did not look like herself. She was on a ventilator and a dialysis machine to try to flush out the poison in her system. Now she was sedated and seemed to be resting peacefully. Someone had put a poison in the water heater of the apartment, and Grandma had been close enough to smell it and ingest it into her lungs. There was no antidote. Grandpa had fared much better as he was not as close to the poison. They brought him down to Grandma's room. Collette asked him if he wanted to tell his wife that he loved her. He just cried, so Collette told Irene that Gideon loves her. Collette stayed with Irene while Larry, and Judy took Gideon back to his room.

Collette told Irene, "I love you so much, Irene. You were always so good to me. You took care of the kids, and you helped me. We don't want you to leave, but if you have to, we will understand. Merl will be waiting for you, and it will be a party with Uncle Art and Uncle Clarence too. Try to relax, and you will have peace."

Then Jenni came into the room, and she told Grandma, "You just have to be here for my wedding, Grandma. I am the last one to get married, and I need you here. I love you, Grandma."

Brad and Desiree came to see Grandma too. Brad just couldn't believe that his grandma was lying there, dying. He did not want to go through loss again. Brad and Desiree went home for the night, but Collette and Jenni stayed at Pat and Curt's house. Larry's family came and other family too.

At 5:00 a.m. on October 1, 2005, Judy called and said that Irene's blood pressure was dropping, so Collette and Jenni were at the hospital a few minutes later. The doctor told them that her brain was probably not working now as she didn't need sedatives and the blood pressure medicine was the only thing keeping her alive. The family went to get Grandpa, but in the meantime, Grandma slipped away. It was 6:50 a.m., and there was a beautiful sunrise. Collette was so upset that she was not with her when she passed away. They did not know it would go that quickly. Larry was so mad and sad and had all these emotions. None of them could believe it. It was hard enough to lose Grandma, but they all knew it was intentionally done by someone who was mentally unstable. They made phone calls and let everyone know. Jenni and Collette left for home. The next few days, they made arrangements for the funeral and for Gideon to be taken to the nursing home.

October 3, 2005

I worked on figuring out where there would be any money for Irene's funeral today. They had a small life insurance policy that will have to do. I went down to talk to Larry about it, but he said he had only fifteen minutes for me. It really struck a raw nerve in me, and I told him that I only have five minutes for him and he was lucky I came down at all today. An hour later, I left. I miss Don so much! I wish he was home. I told him that people die and are buried in five days, and it really happened! I still can't believe any of this has happened. When I left, I didn't want to go home, and I didn't know what to do. The car seemed to drive itself, slowly to Merl's grave. It was such a cold night, and it was dark by then, and the mosquitoes would have been awful. So I just stayed in the car and cried and cried. I have to go through this funeral without Merl. Don came home tonight, and he tried to call me, but my cell phone was dead. He called the house,

and Jenni said there is only one place I could be,
at Dad's grave. I called him when I got home,
and we talked about an hour.

At the funeral, Collette asked Merl's cousin Janice how she let go of Ronnie enough to love someone again. Merl's cousin had been killed by a bull when he was quite young, and his young widow had married again several years later. Janice told Collette, "You just have to follow your heart. Even after all these years, a song or something will trigger it, and I have to cry for Ronnie. That will never end. We never forget the ones we loved, but we can love again and be happy. You have to go on with life."

It was good for Collette to spend time with Merl's family again. All the aunts and uncles and most of the cousins were at the funeral as the family said goodbye to someone who was loved by so many. Later that day, Don was combining beans. He called Collette and asked her to come out and ride along in the combine with him. It felt good to be out in the field, especially after what she had been through.

Later in October, Mike and Joann had Marah Jo. She was a beautiful baby. She ended up in intensive care nursery but soon went home, bringing joy back to the family grieving the loss of their Grandma Schock.

Meanwhile, corn harvest was still in progress. Brad and Collette helped Mike finish up his combining, putting in late nights until it was done. Don kept calling Collette, and she even rode along in his combine a few times too.

Collette was still cleaning at different people's houses. She talked to Luke again when she was there. He said he was trying so hard to move on. He didn't want to be sad anymore.

He wanted to enjoy life again. She told him that is what we all want, but it doesn't just happen; we have to work at it. He always managed to make her laugh when she was there. Time with Luke always felt good.

One night, she got home from cleaning and noticed that there were three cows out. Brad was still at work in Sioux Falls, and she knew she had to get them back in herself. This is the journal entry for that night.

November 16, 2005

When I saw the three cows out, I called Brad right away, but he was still in Sioux Falls, and that meant he was more than an hour away. I started the 1086 and got four pails of corn from Grandpa's bin. I walked out into the field and poured it on the ground. But they were still standing by the gate. I thought maybe they would come for water, so I got a pipe and pounded the ice out of the tank. At first a little spot opened up, but then the ice got thicker, and it was much harder to pound out. As I pounded, my arms got more and more tired. I didn't think I could do it anymore. The cows were crowding around me, and I knew I had to keep going. I couldn't stop. Finally, I said out loud, "Merl, why did you leave me?" And the ice broke just like that. The whole thing broke, and the cows were able to drink the tank. I got away from the cows, and I just cried. I knew Merl had helped me, and I wondered why I don't ask him for help

more often. By now, the cows were standing by
the gate, so I opened it, and they walked right in.

That Thanksgiving, Collette asked Don to come to her sister Pat's house for the meal. He enjoyed time with her family, and Collette loved having the time with her grandchildren, as her whole family attended also.

The days leading up to Christmas were filled with many cleaning jobs and Christmas baking and shopping. Christmas Eve all the kids were gone to their "significant other's" family. So Don came to spend the evening with Collette. She made a candlelight supper, and they opened gifts. He gave her a beautiful white gold necklace. Collette was very happy with it, as she could use it for Jenni's wedding. Then Collette gave Don his gift. It was a JD 4000 precision toy tractor. Don had a 4000 tractor and had been looking for the precision toy. He was amazed and asked where she found it. She said she went to Iowa to get it. Actually, the man from the toy store in LaMar had met her in Sioux Falls, and she bought it. They had a wonderful time together, and it seemed so right. When he left, he told her that it was the best Christmas Eve he ever had.

The next day, Collette went to church. She showed her friends the beautiful necklace she got from Don. She felt lonely as she stayed for church without her family or Don. She wrote in her journal,

December 25, 2005
I looked at the beautiful white poinsettia
in memory of Merl and his mother, and I cried.
I miss them both. I gave the white poinsettia to
Mildred (older lady in the church) and asked

her to take good care of it. She said she would. I went into the sanctuary, and I talked to God. I said, "I know you are having a big celebration up there today, and I am happy that Merl can be there and Irene, and Dad, and Bridget, and all the others. Someday I will come too. But in the meantime, I pray you will give me a little happiness down here." Later the kids all came for a late supper, about 7:30 p.m. It wasn't great, but it was okay. The meal was quiet, as there was just such a large hole in the family. After supper, we opened some presents and played the Newlywed Game. I said it was quite appropriate this year, and I think they enjoyed it. But little Jon got so tired and cried until they had to take him home and put him to bed. I never got to hold Marah all night. At least the holiday is over for this year.

Brad and Mike walked Jenni down aisle at her wedding

Chapter 8

2006 – Finding My Way

Collette and Don spent New Year's Eve with LaVetta and Gayle. They had a good time there and thought the year 2006 held some promise for them. It certainly was better than the last year when Jenni had terrible pain from her wisdom teeth getting dry socket. This year, however, it was Collette's turn at the dentist. Collette had always had a fear of the dentist and consequently had not gone for several years. Don knew it and kept telling her she had to go to the dentist, or she would lose all her teeth. He kept after her to go until finally she made the first appointment. That first appointment was tough, and she was missing Merl so much. She thought about how they had always said if they had each other, they could handle anything. That had worked for Merl, but now she had tough things to face, and he wasn't here. The dentist was very compassionate and said that he could save her teeth if she did the work it would take to get them in shape. She committed to doing it, knowing she would have to face some fears alone, just as she had done with so many other things.

Jenni's wedding was coming up in July, and there were many details to get worked out. Jenni and Collette worked every weekend on wedding plans. Jenni was very good about not spending money, as she was as frugal as her mother.

February 3, 2006

I went to Luke in the morning. He is so sick and acted like he was sleeping on the sofa when I vacuumed. But I saw him open one eye and laugh at me when I couldn't get the mattress on the floor moved with the vacuum cleaner. He is a good man with a very good heart. But Don is the one I have feelings for. In our last conversation, Carrie asked me if I am in love with Don. I got choked up and said, "I think so. It is so scary to say it or even think it." She is scared about a new relationship with a man, too, as she has met someone. In the eve, I went along with Don to a party where I knew a lot of the people. It felt so strange tonight. He sat with the men and talked and I visited with the women. It is like we are a couple, but we are not. I just don't understand all these feelings I have. On the way home from the party, I was very quiet, and Don asked me what was wrong. I said, "I just don't feel right when I was there with all those neighbors who have always known me as the other half of Merl." Then he said, "Tomorrow is Merl's birthday, isn't it?" I started to cry, and I just cried and cried. He didn't know what to do with me until he started to cry with me. I guess

that is what I needed. I just miss Merl so much.
This pain just goes on and on. Why can't I get
past it? He stayed with me for a while and then
left about midnight.

Merl's birthday came and went. It was just another day. Collette went out for supper with her friend Mary. They had a good talk, and Collette felt better.

On Valentine's Day, Collette called Jenni. Collette told Jenni that if Jeff didn't buy her flowers for Valentine's Day, she should not be disappointed. He bought her an expensive ring this year. Jenni asked Collette what she expected from Don. Collette told her that she would be disappointed if she didn't get roses from him for Valentine's day. The minute Jenni got off the phone, she called Don and told him that her mom wanted a dozen red roses for Valentine's Day. But he said it was too late; he already bought her six carnations. When he gave it to Collette, she was disappointed but tried not to show it. They had been at a basketball game for Rachel in Canistota that night.

February 24, 2006

Today I started working for Jason. He is in
a lot of pain. His wife was buried last Sat, and he
was so sick with a cold. He sounded tough with
that deep cough in his chest. He is good-looking,
tall with pretty blue eyes, and about the same
age I am. He seemed pleasant and showed me a
picture of her and said she was petite and thin
and very pretty. I worked there for four hours but
could have spent much more time there in that
large house. His daughter was there and told me

about their family. It is another sad story. Why is it that the good marriages, the happy ones, are broken when someone has to die young? She was only about fifty years old too.

The next day, Collette made a birthday cake for Renae, and they celebrated with friends. Renae loved all the attention. Her birthday is February 29, so she took a lot of teasing that she was only four years old. She was really fourteen. Don went all out to celebrate and made elk steaks for supper. They got the four-wheeler out, and she was very happy, as they all tried to make her feel special. Don took Rachel and Renae home for the night. The next day, he got them again, and brought them to church. Collette sat in the pew with them. Collette took pictures of the girls that day, so Don would have nice pictures of his beautiful girls. He had not had a single picture of them since they left in 2000.

The days flew by, and soon it was April. Collette went to clean at Luke's house. He asked her again to go out to eat lunch in Mitchell. So she said yes. She left her car at Jason's house, so she would not have to drive back to Luke's place. She wanted to start cleaning Jason's house after lunch. Jason's son was working in the yard when Luke showed up with his cool little convertible. Collette was sure it was the first time it felt like a "date" to Luke after his wife had passed away. Jason thought that Collette and Luke were a couple and called Luke later to ask him. Luke declined, saying it was only lunch. Meanwhile, Jason left for a few days, and Collette was left to clean his house.

April 14, 2006

*I cleaned at Jason after Luke, and I had
lunch. It's always fun with Luke. He is such a
character! I got so very tired in Jason's house and
ended up taking a nap on his bed. It was so
soft, and I couldn't help myself (felt a little like
Goldilocks). When I woke up, I went to work
in the bathroom and accidently turned on the
jet air pumps on the tub. But then, I couldn't
figure out how to shut it off. It just wouldn't
let me. I went into panic mode! Finally, I tried
to call Jason on his cell phone, but I suppose
there was no cell service in Nebraska. I had the
drain open and just had to leave it for a while,
hoping Jason would call me back. So I worked
in another room, and suddenly, I heard a loud
noise in the bathroom and came running back.
It sounded like it would take off very soon, so
I hit all the buttons again and finally got it to
shut off. Again, I say, God answers prayers! I
finished cleaning and came home exhausted.*

Don's birthday was the end of April. He got the girls for
the weekend. Collette brought steaks for him to grill, and they
invited their friends Jerry and Barb to come to help celebrate.
Collette gave him a magazine rack for his birthday. She told
him, "As you get older, you will be spending even more time in
the bathroom and will need a magazine rack there for all your
reading material." The box said, "Some assembly required," so
of course, he put the magazine rack together backward. They
all gave him a hard time and said he can't read instructions anymore either. Collette asked Rachel if she would like to drive her

car into town to get gas. Rachel jumped at the chance to drive Collette's car, as she was just sixteen years old. Rachel pushed the gas pedal down too hard and jerked the car, almost hitting Don's car. She giggled and apologized. Later, she accidently beeped the horn. She giggled about that too! They had a good time together.

May 9, 2006

I did some yard work today. I was digging out gravel off the lawn and trying to get weeds out of my flowers. By the time I did more weeds in more flowers, I got mad. I never did like to work on flowers or garden stuff. I only wanted to drive a tractor in the field. Merl understood that. No other woman would have, and I don't know that another man would either, but Merl did. I can't farm with my sons, and I don't know if I can ever farm with Don either. He's such a perfectionist. I wouldn't be able to do it good enough for him. I am so depressed today. My heart aches for Merl and the life we had. We were so poor, but I loved Merl, and I would have kept him and the poverty that surrounded him all my days. Tonight, we give away the scholarship again.

Later—Jenni did a great job giving the scholarship away. I was so proud of her. Don didn't want to go with us, but he called me four times while I was at the FFA meeting. So I called him back. He wanted me to go along

*to Mitchell for supper with him and his friend
Mike. I said I was too tired from working, but
he just insisted, so I went along. It got quite late
by the time we got back. He seemed mad at me
tonight, and I don't have a clue what for. I just
don't think this will ever work out.*

Jenni and Collette and the bridesmaids went to Tyndall to
get the bridesmaids dresses for the first fitting. Jenni looked fantastic, and the red dresses she picked for her bridesmaids were
beautiful. They had a good time trying them on and the trip to
Tyndall was fun too. They also worked on invitations and some
decorations.

May 21, 2006

*Don had Renae only today in church, and I
sat by them. After church, Don invited me to go
along with them to Pizza Ranch. When we got
back to the church, Don and Renae and I walked
over to see Bridget's grave. I had one white rose
left from the decorations for Jenni's wedding. I
told them that would be for Bridget from Don
and the two red roses would be from the sisters.
Don cried when I told him that, and I hope it
meant something to Renae too. She didn't want
to go to Bridget's grave, but Don took her hand
and walked over there. I put a dozen red roses
on Merl's grave, like I always do on Memorial
Day. They came over to Merl's grave too. From
there, they went home, and I did too. Both Brad*

and Mike came in to visit with me a little today. They are trying to plant crop yet. I just feel so distanced from the farming now. They have the girls help them rather than me. It just makes me sad. So I am trying to make my own life and start over. I have forgiven my children for all the tough times we went through, and I pray that they have forgiven me too.

In June, Collette sold some more machinery at the Wieman Auction. It was the rake and the silage cutter. After they said "sold" on the cutter, Collette got all choked up, and tears welled up. She tried to hide it, as she didn't want to make a fool of herself over a piece of machinery. But it was another piece of her life with Merl that was gone. She was selling it, piece by piece. And she knew it had to be, but it still hurt.

June 23, 2006

I went to Luke to clean and then to Jason. Jason wasn't home. Yesterday, he called me to tell me that he is going to Nebraska for the weekend to see his kids and wouldn't be home. He still sounds so depressed. I tried to be encouraging to him, but I know how down he is. In his house, I found the poems that his wife had written. They were passed out at her funeral. I just sat down and cried when I read them. They brought such heartache back again. I was in pain too, so I wrote

Since You're Gone...
by Collette Schock

I keep pretending
I'm okay.
But I'm not.

I keep pretending
I'm handling life without you,
But I'm not.

I keep pretending
I can laugh at jokes again,
But nothing is really funny.

I keep pretending
I can take care of myself,
But I just can't seem to do it.

Still, I keep pretending,
Because when I don't,
It's just too painful.

I left this writing for Jason with a note that said I thought maybe that is how he felt too.

I feel so overwhelmed these days. The wedding is coming, and it will be bittersweet. I will miss Merl so much again. I had thought Don would be there for me to help me get through Jenni's wedding, but tonight I found out differently. He said he doesn't want to go to the rehearsal supper with me and he especially doesn't want to dance with me. That really hurt. It's not like it was asking so very much of him.

The next day, Collette went to a baby shower with Mary, and they stopped at the church and found tablecloths for the wedding and a few other things. It was good to think about the wedding, but Mary knew that Collette was very depressed. In the evening, Collette sat outside on the porch. It was a beautiful night, and it had cooled off. Collette told God, "I don't think Don loves me. Maybe he doesn't understand what real love is. He has had such bad experiences with women, his mother and then his ex-wife. God, I just need someone to love me! I'm so unhappy and so lonely."

The cats on the porch rubbed her legs. She stopped to pet Whitie, a beautiful white cat. He was her favorite. It was almost dark when she noticed a buck walking down the road. It paused by the driveway, and then Collette saw a doe beside the buck. She thought, "Is that my answer? A male and a female deer walking down the road together on a night when I'm asking God if I can have someone in my life? Could it be that He is telling me there is hope? But who would it be? It wouldn't have to be Don."

In July, Don asked Collette to go to his class reunion with him. They had actually graduated the same year but at different schools. Collette graduated from Marion High School, and Don graduated from Salem High School. Collette knew a lot of the people at the reunion and enjoyed being there. Later, they talked, and Collette asked him again if he would dance with her at Jenni's wedding. He said he would, but he felt awkward as he didn't know how to dance very well. She said she would teach him.

July 4, Don and Collette and Rachel and Renae went to a tractor pull. They set up a tent on the back of Don's pickup. It rained a little bit and was cold, but they still enjoyed the day. Collette took food along, and they ate all day. Collette told Don if she had money she would buy a 560 that was really powerful to run, and she would drive it in the tractor pulls. She would have Don be the captain of the pit crew. Don and Mike and Brad would have special T-shirts that said "Redbarn Classic" pit crew, and little Jon would have a T-shirt that said, "I love Grandma's tractor."

"It's only a dream, but it's a fun one. You have to have dreams, or what is life worth?" she said.

July 8, 2006

Jenni's wedding day. We woke up early. Brad stopped for a little while, and Jenni and I visited with him. The bridesmaids were here by 9:00 a.m. and then left to get their hair done. I had mine done last. The girls went directly to the church and got lunch out for everyone. I came home and ate a little yogurt. I was holding up pretty good but had to cry before I left and tell Merl again that I still love him, and I wish he was here. It was so fun to see the church fill up with all the people we love. Don sat about in the middle of the church. Everything went as planned. Jenni was so beautiful and looked so young. Don danced with me three times tonight. The last time was to "Holes in the Floor of Heaven" by Steve Wariner. Brad and Des and Mike and Joann danced to that one too. It was a wonderful night. I pray that Jenni and Jeff will have as deep a love as Merl and I did. I got home at 2:00 a.m. and fell into bed.

A few days later, things were back to normal, and Collette was cleaning houses again. She went to Jason's house, and he had left her a note that he would be home before she got done cleaning. He didn't make it, and after she got home, he called her, just to talk. She thanked him for sending money to Jenni and Jeff for a wedding gift. She had left him a note at his house, saying that his wedding anniversary was coming up. She wrote, "I pray that God will give you the strength you need to get through your anniversary. She still loves you. Love has no boundaries. Hold on to the memories and let God do the rest."

The end of July, one night a storm came over the Schock farm. The wind blew about seventy miles per hour with hail. Collette had put new windows in the house that summer and she was so glad now, as the old ones might have shattered in the fierce wind. It was like a snowstorm. You couldn't see the round bales across from the house. Collette thought the storm was over and was just about to go back to bed when she heard the "train" sound. She ran down the basement and felt her heart pound as she waited under the stairs. After it passed, she couldn't see any damage in the dark, so she went to bed. In the morning light, she could see the machine shed doors damaged. On the other quarter, a calf shelter was thrown on top of the old garage. There were branches down all over. On the way to work, she noticed the neighbor's fields had hail damage, so she came back to look at Brad's. He got hail on his crops and about .60 of rain.

Mike only had .15 and no hail. In the evening, Collette invited Don and Brad/Des and Mike/Jo and family and Jenni/Jeff to come for supper. She told her family, "In 1978, Larry came up here so depressed and said he had lost everything. I asked him if his house is gone and his barn and all the cows. He said no, he got hailed out. Then I told him, Well, thank goodness that is all. It could have been much worse! Perspective, Brad, keep it all in perspective. You will survive this."

The next weekend, Don took his girls to Minneapolis to see a Twins baseball game. They had a great time together, and Don was so happy to finally have his girls again.

Every year, it had been so hard to get through the month of August. Merl and Collette's anniversary was August 18, and Merl died on August 30. Don's daughter Bridget died on August 26, which was also little Jon's birthday. Collette knew that Merl would be so upset with her for missing him so much. He would want her to move on. This year on August 18, Don and Collette went out for supper with LaVetta and Gayle to Sioux Falls. They had a good time together. Gayle said again that he felt like he had met Don in a different life. LaVetta couldn't believe that Don had actually cleaned up his house by himself.

August 30, 2006

Today started off with a bang. I was just ready to leave the house, and the neighbor called and said that Brad's cattle are out on the road. I left with my pickup and called Mike. Thank goodness he was home today to help, because Brad was already at work. Mike and I tried to get them to come out of the neighbors cornfield all morning. Finally, Mike said we have to stop and I have to feed him. So we stopped for dinner. I told him that Dad wants to give us something to do so we don't think about losing him today, and at least Mike and I are together. He agreed. After dinner, Mike went home, and I went to work. In the morning, I was upset again. Merl is in heaven, and I am stuck here in this life. But I heard "Broken Road" by Rascal Flatts on the radio, and I know that Merl is telling me it is okay to go on with life. I talked to Jenni today too. I know she was sad, too, but she seemed okay. I got through today much better than I have. Even our anniversary this year was harder. I suppose the pain lessons with time. I pray that it does, and I know that having Don in my life helps a lot.

Early in September, they got a lot of rain. It rained for two days, and at the end, there was 4.70 in the rain gauge. And they had another inch a few days before that. It was a flood. That Sunday they went to church and in the evening got together for supper. They went to the neighbors to visit a while and, when they got home, made plans to go to another tractor pull. It was heavy on Collette's mind, and finally she asked him, "Don, are we going to end up together or not?"

Don said, "Why do you ask me that?"

"It just feels like we are not going anywhere, not making progress," she said.

Don said, "Your kids take up all your time."

Collette replied, "I think it is more about your girls and what they would think."

He was quite taken back at that and finally said, "I don't know how they will react. I finally got them back in my life, and I don't want to lose them."

"You are not going to lose your girls if I have anything to say about it! They love you and are so happy to finally have you too," Collette replied.

Collette continued, "I'm worried that you had such a bad experience with women, your mom, and ex-wife that maybe you don't want another woman in your life."

Don admitted, "It is really hard to get past that."

"You have to trust me, I'm not like they are."

"I know, and we can work it out," he said.

Then he held her close, kissed her, and told her he loved her.

One night in October, Don called Collette and asked her if she wanted to take a little ride with him. She said yes, so he came up to get her with the old 1995 Ford Pickup. It was a nice evening, about sixty-five degrees and a light breeze.

They went south of her farm, and Collette asked, "Where are we going?"

Don answered, "You will see!" and he flashed her a special smile.

He said, "I'm really lonely over here. Could you come sit by me?"

She moved over slowly to the middle of the older style pickup. By this time, they were closer to his farm. It was dark outside, and she still wondered why he wanted to see her tonight and where they were going. They talked about what they had done that day, and finally they arrived at one of Don's fields. The bean crop was taken off the field, and Don drove right in.

"What are you doing?" Collette asked.

"I want to show you something," Don said.

He drove up to a large lake in the middle of the section. The bright full moon was reflected on the lake, and it looked huge!

Collette said, "It's beautiful. Absolutely beautiful! I don't think I have ever seen a moon that big and reflecting in the water, wow!"

"It's a beautiful moon, a harvest moon on the Big Lake, but not nearly as beautiful as you are right here, right now. I feel like I'm sixteen years old! I love you so much, Collette!" And then he kissed her.

Just then the radio started to play "Mud on the Tires" by Brad Paisley. Listening to this song made Don become a teenager again. He drove out into the field and was driving in circles. They laughed and laughed and had a great time.

Collette wrote in her journal,

> October 10, 2006
> *Don makes me feel like a teenager, and he's sure he's one again too. Maybe, just maybe, this will work after all!*

Harvest continued for all of them. The weather was cooperating, but they had usual amount of breakdowns. Don went to the Black Hills to hunt elk that fall. Collette had some time to think about it all. She wrote in her journal,

> October 19, 2006
> *I couldn't sleep tonight. It occurs to me that maybe the reason I am not sure I want to marry*

Don is I see something of Merl in all these guys I know, and I just don't want to let go of any of that. Luke is like a best friend. We can talk about anything and agree on most of it. Merl and I agreed on almost everything. Jason just lights up my face when I see him. He is such a good, wholesome, honest, giving, and loving man. And his wife was his only love. Merl was like that too. Then there is Aaron. He is a man of great faith, deep thoughts, and he reminded me of what Merl would have been like without me. And Don. Don is the farmer that I always wanted Merl to be. He makes me laugh, and I love that. He is so complex, and colorful. Merl was that too. Don is the one who has won my kids over. They respect him. He loves my grandchildren, simply and honestly. He seems to be the one.

Don's pickup had trouble when he was hunting, and Collette went to get him and his brother from Chamberlain on a Monday. They were so glad to see her. She had rescued them and they knew it. Collette told Don he could use her pickup for farming for a while. Later, she figured out he really wanted it so they could hunt deer, and she felt so used. On the way home from Chamberlain, he asked if she wanted to be dropped off at her house. She said that she needed his car if he was going to use her pickup. She was not about to be just "dropped off." He told her that his brother was staying until Sat. That was when Collette knew they would just be hunting all week. When they got to Don's farm, she got his car and went home. She wrote in journal later that week,

October 31, 2006

Saturday. I was so depressed all day. I have so many things to tell Don, but the whole week has gone by, and I've hardly talked to him. For Halloween tonight, I had only a couple people stop in and just for a few minutes. I realized that years ago when we took the kids trick or treating, it must have really made the neighbors day when we stopped and visited with each one for half an hour! These people today couldn't give me five minutes. Then when Mike and Joann came with Jon and Marah. They only gave me fifteen minutes. They were in such a hurry to leave too. I found out later when they left, they stayed at Tom and Mary for an hour and never did get to all the places they said they were going. That really hurt. They are my grandchildren, and I just wanted a little time with them.

Just before Thanksgiving, Collette found out that Carrie would need surgery, and they didn't know if it was cancer or not. Collette was so upset, and she wrote in her journal,

November 18, 2006

What is with all this cancer? Why is there so much suffering? I don't understand, Lord. I just don't! Please don't let Carrie have cancer. I

love her and need her. She's already suffered so much!

November 19, 2006
I called TSC today, and they have one go-cart left on sale. I took my 1999 Dodge Dakota pickup to Sioux Falls to buy it. When I first saw the blue go-cart, I sat on it and just smiled and giggled. Carrie has to go through this operation, and life is too hard and too short. I need to drive a go-cart!

Don got the go-cart running for Collette. She loved it and drove it till it was almost out of gas. Then she filled it up and drove it again. But they put it away before Collette's kids saw it. It was to be a surprise for Thanksgiving.

When Thanksgiving Day came, Jeff and Jenni loved it. But Brad and Des and Larry seemed to be mad at Collette for spending money. Collette told Brad, "I needed this! My friend Carrie has surgery tomorrow, and she might have cancer. Life is too short without a little fun."

Don's girls, Rachel and Renae, just loved it. They drove it until dark.

Later, Collette found out her friend was okay and didn't have cancer. She was relieved and so happy. A few days later, she went to see Carrie. They had a good visit, and Carrie looked good. On the way home, Collette called Aaron. She told him about Carrie, and they visited awhile. Aaron was very glad to hear from Collette and to hear that their friend was okay.

Jenni was having chest pains off and on before Thanksgiving. Shortly after Thanksgiving, Jenni took a CAT scan to see what was wrong. It seemed a long time to wait for results, but when the report came in, Jenni's heart and everything was okay. That answer told her that stress was still making her feel bad. Soon after finding this out, Collette gave Jenni and Jeff her treadmill and bought a different one, hoping exercise would help Jenni.

Collette helped Mike dig in railroad ties. She wrote in her journal,

November 28, 2006

I did maid work in the morning and then took the pm off to help Mike. It was a nice day, still warm. Mike and I dug RR ties in his cow yard. He dug them, and I pulled dirt away from digger. We got fifteen holes dug and most of the RR ties put in. One of the ties fell on me till Mike came and rescued me. Once he said not to come near because there was a mouse in the hole. He used a tiny pliers all day, and I could hardly stand to see him gnaw off the wire with it. You need proper tools to do fencing. Then we went inside for coffee and rolls. It was a good day for Mike. I think he actually liked working with Mom, but I'll bet he would never admit it! Your mom is your biggest fan, and sometimes you just need that.

November 29, 2006

Got up and went to work. Then stopped at Cenex and got two pair of gloves, one for Mike and one for Joann. From there, I went to Mitchell and bought Mike a bolt cutter, a

fencing pliers and a regular pliers. On the way home, I stopped at Mike's and put the tools and gloves in his house with a ribbon and said, "To Mike and Joann from Santa." Later I found out I had accidently locked the house and they had to get in from the basement because they couldn't remember where they put the outside key!

December was busy with cleaning jobs, as people wanted their houses clean for the holidays. Collette enjoyed making Christmas goodies for each of her customers. She got many very nice Christmas presents also.

December 18, 2006

I cleaned houses all day, and then Don wanted me to come there for supper, but I had to bring it along. So I took some chicken rice soup, and he got it all heated up. He insisted that I drink some milk. I told him I don't like white milk, so he got out some ovaltine to make it chocolate. He filled his glass with milk, and then while he talked to me, he carefully sprinkled ovaltine over his entire bowl of soup. I watched him do it and then burst out laughing. We both laughed and laughed. It was great. I sat on his lap then and told him I loved him. I said it is so good to be with him because he understands my grief. Because we both have experienced loss, we know how to comfort each other. Later he said the running boards on my pickup were about $369 plus tax and installation. I said *that's too much and he should just forget it. A few days earlier, I had teasingly said something like, "If I'm not getting a ring for Christmas, I want running boards on my pickup." So then he immediately took my pickup to town to measure it. I don't think I'm getting a ring for Christmas.*

Don came to Collette's house for Christmas Eve supper. It was just the two of them. They had a wonderful candlelight supper. Don really liked it and shut off all the lights except the candles on the table. This, of course, made it almost impossible to see what you were eating. They enjoyed each other's company, but there was no engagement ring. Collette was okay with that. She knew by now that it is all about God's timing, and if Don was not ready for it, it was best they wait. She was still not completely sure either if it was the right thing to do.

December 25, 2006
Christmas Day
I worked all day, cleaning and getting food ready. I had the radio on with Christmas music, and it was a good day. I lit the candle on the kitchen table, and when they played "Angels Among Us" by Alabama, the flame was so high. I knew Merl's spirit was present. So Merl and I had a good day preparing for the family. I kept praying that God would let our family have a good time together. And He did. Don and the girls came first and then Mike's family. It was so good to see the kids. Jon can talk so much more now. We played all night, but I did get to do a

few things with the family too. Renae was so good with the little kids. She also liked the computer, and Rachel was playing piano a lot. She is very good and has only had two lessons. Those girls have missed so much in their lives. Jenni and Jeff got here just before 6:00 p.m., and then Brad and Des were last. They had to make the macaroni salad. It only had miracle whip and macaroni. Jenni dug around in it and asked where the rest of it was! Everyone was in a good mood, and we had a good time. The little kids were such good entertainment. Jon loved the skidloader like "Maamaa's" (Grandma's). He and Brad played with it all night. Even Mike was in a good mood. It was great! The kids left about 9:30 p.m., but Don and the girls stayed until after 11:00 p.m. I actually got to talk to Rachel a little bit. She is so sweet. And I think Renae is coming around too. They actually liked the blankets I made for them. When they left, they came and gave me a big hug. I didn't have to do it first! It was great! Don called about 12:30 when he got home. He was so happy that he had the day with the girls and liked being up here with me because he could talk to them so easily that way. It was a good Christmas.

After Christmas, Collette went to Luke to clean. They had a good time talking about Christmas and the family. She knew that he was doing better and had enjoyed his family over the holidays.

For New Years Eve, LaVetta and Gayle came to play pinochle. They all had a good time, and LaVetta caught on quickly. Jenni and Jeff came out for a while—until they had lunch and then left. The four of them played more cards after that, and the new year came in quietly. Collette wondered what the new year would hold. In 2007, it would be five years since Merl is gone. She hoped for a good year with happiness for not only her, but her family too.

Don & Collette

Chapter 9

2007 – The End of the Broken Road

There was always a lot of maid work to do, but occasionally, Collette made time to go and visit Larry and Judy. On one such occasion, Collette asked Larry if he had been able to forgive the man responsible for his mother's death, two years earlier. Larry immediately got very upset and said, "Hell, *no!*" Collette tried to talk to him about it.

She told him, "Merl forgave your dad for all the alcoholism and pain that it brought. And your dad never even asked for forgiveness. Forgiving others releases us from anger and allows us the healing we need. We make a choice to forgive. When we forgive, we have peace."

"I'm never going to forgive him! He took Ma away!" Larry replied.

"Forgiveness doesn't justify action or provide God's forgiveness. God is the only one who can do that. But it is so important to forgive others. It talks about it in Matthew that if we forgive others, our Heavenly Father will forgive us, but if we do not forgive others, God will not forgive us. Larry, you need to forgive him. Give it all over to God and let Him take care of it."

"No, I can't do that!" said Larry, and he turned away as if it was time for Collette to leave.

"Merl had time to think about all these things before he died and make things right. But you might not get that time," said Collette, but she could see that it was best that she go home.

So she left, apologizing to Judy that she got Larry all riled up. She didn't know when or if he did forgive, only knowing it was a struggle for him. She wished she could help him through this, as she knew he probably still had anger toward his father for the alcoholism too.

Don continued to be a part of Collette's life. She went with him to ball games and volleyball games that his girls were involved in. He went with her to see the grandkids at Mike and Joann's house. Mike ended up buying Don's planter and was very happy with it. Don and Collette talked on the phone every day.

Collette decided in January that she would sell her stock cows. Brad wanted to buy some, and a friend also wanted to buy some. Brad had been after her for a while already to sell him the cows. They had been calf crop sharing, but Brad wanted to own them. So Collette set up a contract with him so he could buy them. At first, Collette was not happy with having to let them go. Finally, she realized that she could not take care of them the way she once did, now that she was working so many hours. Brad was so young and energetic and wanted it very much. So she felt it was right to sell them to him.

January 22, 2007

I got up late but still did fifteen min on the treadmill. Then went to SF to meet Char for lunch. I got a gift for Luke's birthday. I hope he likes it. Char and I had such a good time today. Jenni ended up coming out to my house tonight. I kept her busy all night going through boxes, etc.

January 28, 2007

I got to church late because Brad stopped for coffee. I hate to tell him I have to leave. Don had the girls in church today. We sang "Power of Your Love" in church today, and I cried. Renae asked why I was crying, and I told her that was one of the songs at Merl's funeral. She hugged me. The girls have been so sweet to me. We had a guest preacher in church today. He was blind, and he gave a wonderful message. He talked about how Peter walked on the water, and as long as he focused on Jesus, he was okay, but the minute he took his eyes off Jesus, he started to sink. Then Jesus took his hand and brought him back up. The minister told us to reach for things that seem impossible because with God all things are possible. And maybe that impossible thing is just what God wanted you to do. He talked about how God asked him to move to SD from Indianapolis where everything was comfortable. It made me think again how much I want to write this book. Maybe it will be a reality. I just need to believe it will be. Don and I talked about it later. I told Don that I know what I said and did helped Merl go to heaven in peace. I kept telling him he is the lucky one. He gets to go to heaven. I would trade places with him in an instant, and I really meant it. I think that made it easier for Merl to go. Don said that Merl knew he was really loved by me and by God. I know that is true.

Collette went with Don to Rachel and Renae's parents night for basketball. The girls were so happy he was there and gave him a big hug. Rachel had told one of her friends that she came home from Dad and couldn't wait until she could go back again. Don was so happy to hear that!

February 14, 2007

It was -27 degrees this morning, so I was a half-hour late for work all day. It was a long day, and I called Don and left a message for him that I was running late. I knew he went to the eye doctor today, and I had a bad feeling about it from the time he mentioned it. He had said that his eye got so tired reading a book on Monday. When I finally got to his house, he was all ready to take me out for supper. But then he said it. He said he got bad news at the eye doctor in town. He said that he has a mole in the back of his eye. It doesn't look bad now, but the doctor thinks it might be growing from two or three years ago when they looked at it last. They want him to take a picture of it at the clinic in two weeks. He said that a lot of people have it and never even know it, but one in nineteen thousand people have it turn into cancer. I was hit like a ton

of bricks. Half of what he said I didn't hear. I
didn't want to fall apart, but I did, anyway. I
cried and told him that I love him and nothing
can happen to him. All the while I was thinking,
"This can't be happening! It can't happen twice
in one lifetime!" When I got a hold of myself, I
told him it is not the same thing as Merl. Merl
had melanoma, and they knew it right away.
Don did not seem to be too worried about it.
He knew the picture was so they can watch if it
grows or not. He would take another picture in
a couple of months. Don knew he could end up
blind, as the mole was in his good eye. Then he
said he got roses for me. He went into another
room and brought out six red roses for me. (I
was thinking, "Only six? Where is a dozen!")
I read the card, and it said, "Be Mine." Then
he said I should look closer. Under the card on
the rose leaves was a beautiful diamond ring. I
took it out of there (quick, before it fell into the
water), and by then, he was down on one knee,
asking me to marry him. I said, "Yes!" He still
took me to Red Lobster tonight, and we talked
about when we could get married and tried to
make some plans. I am so very happy!

Collette wrote in her journal,

February 15, 2007
Don finally did it! He asked me to marry
him! I know now he is finally ready for it. He is

ready for our life together. And I know it is right. I feel Merl's blessing on it. I know that Merl never said I should get married again, because it was just too painful to think about. But I know he would not have wanted me to be alone for half of my life if he couldn't be here with me. Real love is like that. You would give up anything for the other one. I feel very blessed. When I called Don today, he was depressed thinking about his eye. He said it is so overwhelming. We should just be so happy now and nothing else, and now we have this hanging over us. I thought about it all day. Finally, I decided that when you love someone, you stick with them. I want Don, and I want as much time together with him as I can get. I told Brad today, and he was so happy for us. I told him I will miss all the coffee times with him. He said he will miss that too. After I talked to Brad, I called Mike to tell him. He seemed pleased also and said it was only a matter of time. Mike called Don later to congratulate him. I waited for Jenni to come home from her job tonight. I made up an excuse for her to come out. At first, I waved the ring around, and she didn't notice. Finally, she asked how Don did for Valentine's Day. Then I showed her the ring, and she almost fell over. When she got herself together, she sat down at the kitchen table, folded her hands, and said, "I would like to offer my services as a wedding planner for only $100/hr!" She was so sweet *and funny! She asked what the grandkids will call Don. I told her I thought maybe Grandpa Don. I said I want my grandchildren to know who their Grandpa Merl is, but I know that Grandpa Don will be here to love them.*

The five children were all very happy that Don and Collette were going to get married. They all had a great time being involved in making plans. They planned a very private ceremony at Sun Prairie Baptist Church, followed by an open-house reception. Collette asked Don when there was no hunting season so that they could have a wedding and she could have an anniversary every year. They decided on September 8, 2007 (9-8-7). She figured she might have half a chance for him to remember that one!

In May, Jenni graduated from college with a teaching degree. Collette remembered how Jenni had left for college the day after the funeral. She had dealt with so many stress attacks and other problems at college, but she had persevered, and now she was graduating. Collette was so very proud of her and again wished Merl was here for this very special day. She knew how proud he would be of her for graduating, and especially with a degree in Education. Collette knew she would be a very good teacher.

The family had a great time together that summer. Rachel and Renae liked the idea of siblings and already adored their nephew and niece. Joann was pregnant with another child, due in September soon after the wedding. Jenni was getting more sisters, something she always wanted. Mike and Brad were very protective older brothers to Rachel and Renae, and no guys better be messing with their sisters, or they would have to answer to the two of them! Two very broken families were coming together, and they were happy again, making the best out of life.

August 30, 2007

Today is five years that Merl is gone. It is a mountain I have crossed. I have learned so much through all of this. God is real. There is no doubt! God has been with me every step of the way, and He has tried to teach me how to live, how to love, and how to forgive. These are basic to life here on earth. If we totally give everything over to God, He will take care of us. We are all on a journey of faith until we can go home to God, as Merl did.

September 7, 2007

I only have one day left! I will miss Brad stopping for coffee or a pop. I will miss my house and the peace and comfort I have here. I will miss the neighborhood and all my friends here. I will miss this farm. But I know I have so much to gain too. I will have someone to make me laugh and have fun with. I will have a new house project that will take years to complete. (Maybe that is not on the plus side!) But I also think it is part of God's plan. We are bringing healing to two very broken families. Tonight when we had all the kids together for supper, it was so good for all of them, and they had a great time together. I

still love Merl. That will never change, but I can
love Don too, and it will be good.

The time went by quickly, and the wedding day arrived. It was a beautiful fall day. Jenni was maid of honor; Rachel and Renae were bridesmaids. Don had his brother as best man, Mike and Brad as groomsmen. Little Jon and Marah ran up to Mike and wanted him to hold them as they started the ceremony. Everyone was dressed so nice and looked so happy. The song "Bless the Broken Road" by Rascal Flats (written by Marcus Hummon, Bobby Boyd, and Jeff Hanna) played as Collette walked down the aisle. The words of the song are very true. Sometimes in life we get lost on the broken road, but God will always be there to lead us back.

Summary

I t is now 2018 and it has taken me all these years to write this. At first it just hurt too much to write it, and I struggled through the pain all over again. But timing is all up to God. Only He knows when the time is perfect.

Don and I are married over ten years. His eye is just fine, and we are still farming. I retired from maid work in 2013. We have eleven beautiful grandchildren. Rachel and Renae are not married yet, so there is the potential of having more! God has blessed us. Don also made good on his promise of a real boat for me, and we have enjoyed boating very much.

When you go through all the trials and troubles in life, you must hang on to your faith. God is real! I have felt His touch, felt Him leading me, teaching me. He never sent me the email I was always looking for, but He was still there with me and continues to be. Bad things are going to happen in life here on earth. They are only an opportunity to show God that we do have faith in Him, and we love and trust Him. Because we all sin, we need to be willing to forgive others. Forgiveness is the ultimate symbol of love. To love unconditionally (no matter what) is what Jesus taught us, and what God wants from us. God is always there with open arms when we choose to come back to Him.

You may contact me at my email address – collettecarlson2@gmail.com

If you would like to find out more about God and a Bible-based church, please contact us at Sun Prairie Baptist Church near Salem, South Dakota. The website is www.sunprairiebaptist.com.

Bibliography

Ewing, Skip, and Donny Kees, writers. "I Believe." In *16 Biggest Hits*. Diamond Rio. Arista Nashville, 2002, compact disc.

Don & Collette Carlson September 8, 2007

Schock Carlson Family September 8, 2007

Back row – L-R Joann Schock, Brad and
Desiree Schock, Rachel Carlson
Middle row – L-R Mike Schock holding Marah and
Jon; Collette and Don Carlson, Renae Carlson
Front Row – Jenni and Jeff Heumiller

Schock Carlson Family 2017

Back row – L-R Mike, Joann, Jon, Rachel, Nate, Renae,
Next row – L-R Jeff, Jenni holding Courtney, Brad and Desiree
Next row- L-R Marah, Collette holding
Zane, Mandi, Don holding Hannah
Front row – L-R Hailey, Sydney, Sadie, Addi, and Lexi

About the Author

Collette Carlson is a farmer from Salem, SD. She has always felt it is a privilege to care for this beautiful earth that God has given us. She loves to drive tractor and watch the crops grow. Family gatherings at the Carlson house are full of love and laughter. When Collette married Don, her family of two sons and one daughter grew with the addition of Don's two daughters. Their family has now grown to twenty-three. Her eleven grandchildren are the joy of Collette's life and give her volumes to write about. Journaling and writing have been a large part of her life, as she started writing when she was very young. She has written many poems and short stories about her children when they were growing up on the farm. Collette is often asked to work with people one-on-one who are struggling with grief. Her own experience has inspired people to remain strong in their faith. She is active in her church and has served in leadership positions.

CPSIA information can be obtained
at www.ICGtesting.com
Printed in the USA
FFHW021756310319
51357456-56829FF